AN INTRODUCTION TO
PAINTING IN
WATERCOLOR
HAZEL HARRISON

AN INTRODUCTION TO
PAINTING
IN
WATERCOLOR
HAZEL HARRISON

A QUINTET BOOK

Published by Chartwell Books
A Divison of Book Sales, Inc.
110 Enterprise Avenue
Secaucus, New Jersey 07094

ISBN 1-55521-069-4

This book was designed and produced by
Quintet Publishing Limited
6 Blundell Street
London N7

Art Director: Peter Bridgewater
Designer: Ian Hunt
Editors: Shaun Barrington, Robert Stewart
Photographer: Ian Howes
Picture researcher: Andrew Kidd

Typeset in Great Britain by
Central Southern Typesetters, Eastbourne
Manufactured in Hong Kong by
Regent Publishing Services Limited
Printed in Hong Kong by Leefung-Asco Printers Limited

CONTENTS

Introduction	7
Materials and equipment	13
Technique	25
Basic rules for artists	37
Landscape and seascape	49
Buildings	69
Nature	81
Portrait and figure	101
Still-life	115
Glossary	124
Index	126

CHAPTER ONE

INTRODUCTION

The main body of Samuel Palmer's work was in oil. It was highly accomplished, but uninspired. His early watercolours, drawings and etchings, however, were works of true poetic imagination and owed much to the influence of William Blake, whom he met in 1824. Paintings such as the one shown here, The Magic Apple Tree, *have their starting points in nature, but go far beyond it to create dream-like fantasy worlds, personal visions expressed in strange, emotive colours and almost Expressionist brush work. Unlike the 18th-century watercolourists, Palmer used semi-opaque paint. But his handling of it was so sure that the colours never became muddy or muted, as they often do with gouache paints in less skilful hands.*

'I DON'T DO WATERCOLOUR; it's far too difficult' is a remark often heard from amateur painters, even those who regard themselves as reasonably proficient in other media, such as oils. It cannot be denied that some people find watercolours a little harder to use than oils. This very attractive medium is sometimes unpredictable, but this very unpredictability should be regarded as a virtue, not a drawback. What people really mean when they make this kind of remark is that watercolours cannot be altered over and over again as oils can; a colour or wash, once laid down on the paper, must stay there. To some extent this is true, and it is understandable that people should feel a certain nervousness when approaching a watercolour. But, in fact, many alterations can be made, and often are, as a painting progresses: a wash in a colour that has not come out quite right can be changed dramatically by applying another wash on top of it; areas can be sponged out or worked over; and if the worst comes to the worst the whole painting can be put under running water and washed away.

Watercolour has many virtues, its main attraction for artists being its freshness and translucence, making it ideal for a variety of subjects, especially landscapes and flower paintings. As its name implies, pure watercolour is mixed with water and is transparent, so that it must be applied from light to dark, unlike oil paint or acrylics which are opaque and can be built up from dark to light. Highlights consist of areas of the paper left white or very pale washes surrounded by darker ones. A certain amount of pre-planning is necessary at an early stage to work out where the highlights are to be, but some planning is always needed for any painting or drawing, whatever medium is being used.

No one ever quite knows how watercolour will behave, and many watercolour artists find this very unpredictability one of its greatest assets. The medium itself will often begin to 'take over' a painting, suggesting ways of creating interesting effects and lending a sparkle and spontaneity to the work. Experience is needed to make the most of the chance effects that occur in watercolour painting. A real feeling for the medium may not be achieved until several attempts have been abandoned, but there are many ways of using watercolour and with perseverance you will evolve your own style and method. The purely practical advantages of watercolour painting are that you need little expensive equipment, the painting can be done more or less anywhere provided there is enough light, and paints can be cleared up quickly, leaving no mess. Since the paper is relatively cheap, experiments and mistakes are not very expensive.

◆ THE MEDIUM ◆

Watercolour, like all paint, is made by mixing pigment with a binding agent, in this case gum arabic, which is soluble in water. There are two types of watercolour, 'pure' or 'classical' watercolour, which is transparent, and gouache, or 'body colour', which is the same pigment made opaque by adding white pigment to the binder. The

ABOVE *John Sell Cotman was the leading watercolourist of the 18th-century British School. In paintings like this one,* St Benet's Abbey, Norfolk, *he used paint in a bold, free and imaginative way to create marvellous effects of space, light and texture. Notice particularly the broad, overlapping brush strokes in the foreground and the swirling, directional ones in the sky.*

technique of gouache painting is similar to that of oil or acrylic, since light colour can be laid over dark, and is outside the scope of this book; but gouache is quite frequently used in conjunction with pure watercolour. Its use is a source of constant controversy among water-colourists: some claim that it destroys the character of the medium — its luminosity — and should never be used; others combine the two with considerable success. Nowadays there is a general trend towards mixing differ-ent media, and watercolour is often used with pastel, pen and ink, pencils or crayons (see Chapter 3). It can be a

useful exercise, when a watercolour has 'gone wrong', to draw into it with inks or pastels to see the effects that can be achieved.

◆ THE HISTORY OF ◆ WATERCOLOUR PAINTING

It is commonly believed that watercolour was invented by the English landscape painters of the 18th century, but this is far from so. Watercolour has been in use in various

John Sell Cotman worked on a fairly small scale, but his landscapes and seascapes give an impressive feeling of space, strength and power, and are extraordinarily modern in approach. Many have an almost abstract quality, as in this painting, The Dismasted Brig,

where the rain-swept sky has been treated in bold, broad masses, and the swirling movement of the waves has been used to make a geometric pattern of different-sized triangles.

RIGHT Albrecht Dürer, who painted this painting, which has come to be known as The Great Piece of Turf, *found watercolour a particularly sympathetic medium for detailed studies of nature. We cannot be sure of his precise method, but he probably began by*

using transparent washes to establish broad areas, such as the large leaves, and then built up intricate details with tiny strokes of opaque paint (or body colour).

forms for many centuries. Indeed the ancient Egyptians used a form of it for painting on plaster to decorate their tombs; the great frescoes of Renaissance Italy were painted in a kind of watercolour; it was used by medieval manuscript illuminators, both in its 'pure' form and mixed with body colour; the great German artist, Albrecht Dürer (1471-1528), made use of it extensively, and so did many botanical illustrators of the 16th century and the Dutch flower painters of the 17th century.

It was, even so, in 18th-century England that watercolour painting was elevated to the status of a national art. A new interest in landscape painting for its own sake culminated in the work of John Constable (1776-1837), the forerunner of the Impressionists. Landscape had hitherto been purely topographical — a truthful and detailed record of a particular place — but in the hands of artists such as Paul Sandby (1725-1809), John Cozens (1752-97), Thomas Girtin (1775-1802), Francis Towne (1740-1816), John Sell Cotman (1782-1842) and Peter de Wint (1784-1849) it became much more than that. Watercolour was at last fully exploited and given the recognition that was its due.

Most of these artists worked in watercolour alone, regarding it as the perfect medium for creating the light, airy, atmospheric effects they sought; Constable used watercolour mainly for quick sketches of skies. The greatest watercolourist of all, J M W Turner (1775-1851), achieved his fame as an oil painter, but he produced watercolours of an amazing depth and richness. Quite

uninhibited by any 'rules', he exploited accidental effects like thumbprints and haphazard blobs of paint, turning them into some of the most magical depictions of light and colour that have ever been seen in paint.

Throughout the 19th century the techniques of watercolour continued to be developed and the subject matter became more varied. The poet and artist, William Blake (1757-1827), evolved his own method of conveying his poetic vision in watercolour, as did his follower, Samuel Palmer (1805-81), who used swirls and blocks of opaque colour in his visionary and symbolic landscapes. With the end of the Napoleonic Wars in 1815, travel once again became easier, and the topographical tradition reached new heights in the work of artists like Samuel Prout (1783-1852), a superlative draughtsman who painted the buildings and scenery of western Europe in faithful detail. Travelling further afield, John Frederick Lewis (1805-76) made glowing studies of Middle Eastern scenes, and new techniques, such as the 'dragged' wash, were pioneered by Richard Parkes Bonington (1802-28) for both landscape and figure subjects, to be taken further by his friend, the French artist, Eugène Delacroix (1798-1863).

British artists of the 20th century have not ignored the possibilities of watercolour, its greatest exponents being Graham Sutherland (1903-80) and Paul Nash (1889-1946) and his brother John (1893-). It remains a popular medium with both professional artists and amateurs, and new ways are constantly being found of exploring its full potential.

CHAPTER TWO

MATERIALS AND EQUIPMENT

*This paintbox might be regarded by some as messy, but this
artist finds that he achieves a greater unity of colour by
allowing traces of old colour to remain on the palette. He
cleans the mixing trays only when the colours become
muddied or when a different range of colours is required.*

Payne's grey and cadmium yellow.

Prussian blue and cadmium yellow.

Cobalt and cadmium yellow.

Prussian blue and lemon yellow.

Viridian and lemon.

Black and cadmium yellow.

Cobalt blue and alizarin crimson.

Payne's grey and alizarin crimson.

Prussian blue and alizarin crimson.

Cobalt blue and Payne's grey.

Black and Prussian blue.

Black and alizarin crimson.

Cadmium yellow and cadmium red.

Alizarin crimson and cadmium yellow.

Lemon yellow and cadmium red.

Burnt umber and black.

Payne's grey and cadmium red.

Burnt umber and cobalt blue.

ERHAPS THE GREATEST single advantage of watercolour painting is that only a small amount of equipment is needed, equipment which is easy to store. Paints and brushes, although not cheap, last for a long time; indeed brushes should last virtually for ever if looked after properly. Hand-made paper is, of course, expensive, but beginners will find that many perfectly satisfactory machine-made papers are available from artist's suppliers.

◆ PAINTS AND COLOURS ◆

Ready-made watercolour paint is sold in various forms, the commonest being tubes, pans and half-pans. These all contain glycerine and are known as semi-moist colours, unlike the traditional dry cakes, which are still available in some artist's suppliers, but are not much used today. Dry cakes require considerable rubbing with water before the colour is released. It is a slow process, but the paints are therefore economical.

Gouache paints, or designer's colours as they are sometimes called, are normally sold in tubes. These paints, and the cheaper versions of them, poster colours and powder paints, have chalk added to the pigment to thicken it, and are thus opaque, unlike true watercolour. Watercolours themselves can be mixed with Chinese white to make them opaque or semi-opaque, so that they become a softer and more subtle form of gouache.

Success in watercolour painting depends so much on applying layers of transparent, but rich, colour that it is a mistake to buy any but the best-quality paints, known as 'artist's quality'. There are cheaper paints, sold for 'sketching', but since these contain a filler to extend the pigment, the colour is weaker and the paint tends to be chalky and unpredictable in use.

Whether to use pans, half-pans or tubes is a personal choice. Each type has its advantages and disadvantages. Tubes are excellent for those who work mainly indoors on a fairly large scale, as any quantity of paint can be squeezed out of them on to the palette. Any paint left on the palette after a painting is completed can be used again later, simply by moistening it with a wet brush. Pans and half-pans, which can be bought in sets in their own palette and are easy to carry, are the most popular choice for working out of doors on a small scale. Watercolours can also be bought in concentrated form in bottles, with droppers to transfer the paint to the palette. These are eminently suitable for broad washes which require a large quantity of paint, but they are less easy to mix than the other types.

The choice of colours is also personal, though there are some colours that everyone must have. Nowadays there is such a vast range of colours to choose from that a beginner is justified in feeling somewhat bewildered, but, in fact, only a few are really necessary. One point to bear in mind is that some colours are considerably less permanent than

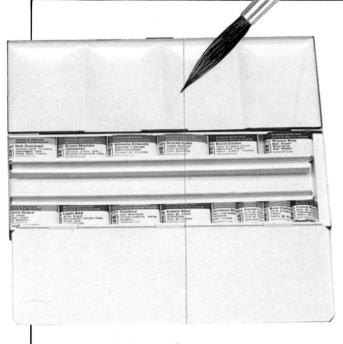

ABOVE A pocket set of watercolours is particularly useful when painting out of doors, or when travelling.

LEFT: These swatches show some of the effects that can be achieved by mixing in a limited colour range.

ABOVE Semi-moist pans must be carried in tins and boxes, which can then be used as palettes.

BELOW MIDDLE Half pans are available individually as well as in sets. The artist can replace the most frequently used colours, and also build up a palette to suit his own style.

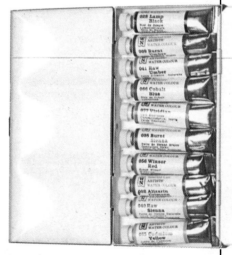

ABOVE Bottled watercolours are concentrated, and quicker to use than dry cakes or semi-moist pans when a large area of wash is required.

RIGHT Watercolour in tube form is popular and convenient. Do not squeeze too many colours onto your palette at a time, or they will run together.

LEFT Gouache is available in tube or pot form in an enormous range of colours. From left to right: lamp black, zinc white, burnt sienna, raw umber, yellow ochre, cadmium red (pale) cadmium yellow (pale), Winsor emerald, cobalt blue.

others, which may not be an important consideration for quick sketches and 'note-taking', but clearly is for any painting that is intended to be hung or exhibited. A wise course, therefore, is to rule out any colours classified as 'fugitive'. All the major paint manufacturers have systems of grading permanence. These are not always marked on the tubes or pans, but they appear on the manufacturers' colour charts; if in doubt, ask the shopkeeper or manager for advice. The tubes or pans will also bear a code indicating the relative price of each colour, some being more expensive than others according to the cost of the pigment used.

The golden rule when choosing a range of colours, or 'palette' as professionals call it, is to keep it as simple as possible. Few watercolourists use more than a dozen colours. For landscape painting, useful additions to the basic palette are sap green, Hooker's green, raw umber and cerulean blue, while monastral blue (called Winsor blue in the Winsor and Newton range) is sometimes recommended instead of Prussian blue. For flower painting the basic range might be enlarged by the addition of cobalt violet and lemon yellow.

◆ PAPER ◆

The traditional support — the term used for the surface on which any painting is done — is white or pale-coloured paper, which reflects back through the transparent paint to give the translucent quality so characteristic of watercolours. There are many types of watercolour paper. Each individual will probably need to try several before establishing which one suits his method of working, though sometimes a particular paper may be chosen to create a special effect.

The three main types of machine-made paper are hot-pressed (HP), cold-pressed (CP), which is also rather quaintly known as 'not' for 'not hot-pressed' and rough. Hot-pressed paper is very smooth and, although suitable

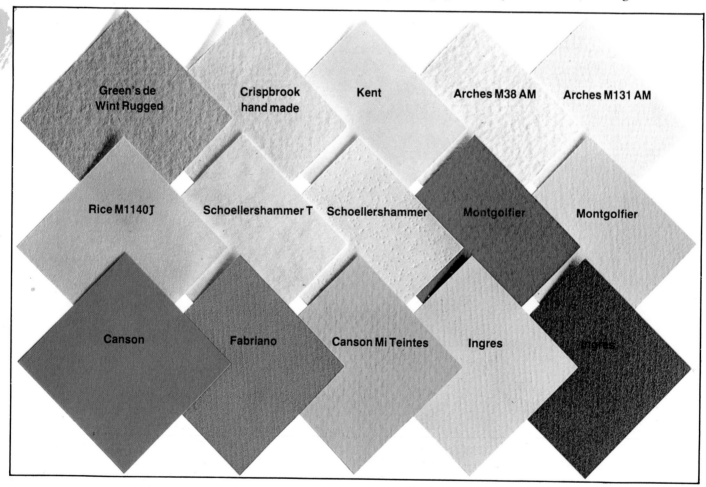

Green's de Wint Rugged

Crispbrook hand made

Kent

Arches M38 AM

Arches M131 AM

Rice M1140J

Schoellershammer T

Schoellershammer

Montgolfier

Montgolfier

Canson

Fabriano

Canson Mi Teintes

Ingres

Ingres

ABOVE The range of papers available is vast and can be bewildering even for the experienced artist. In order to find the paper which suits your particular style and immediate needs, buy only a few sheets at a time. The heavier papers are more expensive but can absorb large amounts of water; they do not, therefore, need stretching, which makes them useful for outdoor work. Toned papers provide a convenient middle ground for some subjects, from which to work darks and lights.

for drawing or pen-and-wash, is not a good choice for building up layers of washes in the standard watercolour technique as it becomes clogged very quickly. Cold-pressed paper, which is slightly textured, is the most popular and is suitable for both broad washes and fine detail. Rough paper, as its name implies, is much more heavily textured, and the paint will settle in the 'troughs' while sliding off the 'peaks', giving a speckled effect which can be effective for some subjects but is difficult to exploit successfully. Among the best-known makes of good watercolour papers are Saunders, Fabriano, Arches, Bockingford, Strathmore in the US, Ingres in the UK, and R.W.S. (Royal Watercolour Society), some of which also include hand-made papers.

Hand-made papers are made from pure linen rag and specially treated with size to provide the best possible surface for watercolour work. Such papers are sized on one side only and thus have a right and a wrong side, which can be checked by holding the paper up to the light so that the watermark becomes visible. Many of the better machine-made papers also have a watermark and hence a right and wrong side.

Some papers have surfaces which are tough enough to withstand a great deal of preliminary drawing and rubbing out without damage, but others do not. Bockingford paper, for instance, although excellent in many ways, is quickly damaged by erasing, and the paint will take on a patchy appearance wherever the surface has been spoiled. One of its advantages, however, is that paint can easily be removed by washing out where necessary; the paint, moreover, can be manipulated and moved around in a very free way. Arches paper and Saunders paper are both strong enough to stand up to erasing, but mistakes are difficult to remove from the former, which holds the paint very firmly. Saunders paper is a good choice for beginners: it is strong, stretches well and has a pleasant surface with enough grain to give a little, but not too much, texture.

♦ STRETCHING THE PAPER ♦

Watercolour papers vary widely in weight, or thickness, and the lighter ones need to be stretched or they will buckle as soon as wet paint is applied to them. The weight is usually expressed in pounds and refers to the weight of a ream (480 sheets), not to each individual sheet. The thinner papers, ranging from 70 to 140 pounds, must be stretched; any paper weighing 200 pounds or more can be used without this treatment. Watercolour boards can be bought. These have watercolour paper mounted on heavy board, so that the stretching has already been done. They are particularly useful for outdoor work, since no drawing board is needed.

Stretching paper is not difficult, but since the paper must be soaked, it takes some time to dry thoroughly and needs to be done at least two hours before you intend to start work. Cut the paper to the size required (if you do not want to use the whole sheet) and wet it well on both sides by laying it in a bath or tray of water. When it is well soaked, hold it up by the corners to drain off the excess

STRETCHING PAPER.

1. *Cut the paper to size and place it right-side up in a bath or tray of water. Leave it to soak for a few minutes.*

2. *Lift out the paper and drain off the excess water.*

3. *Lay the paper on a drawing board at least 1 in/2.5 cm larger than the paper all around. Make sure that the paper is still the right way up.*

4. *Smooth the paper quite flat and stick gumstrip around the edges, starting with opposite sides.*

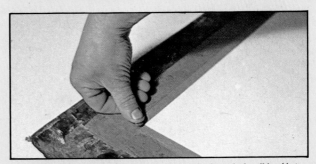

5. *Finish by putting a drawing pin in each corner. Do not dry the paper in front of a fire, which will buckle it.*

water, then lay it right-side-up on a drawing board and stick down each edge with the gummed brown paper known as gumstrip (do not use masking tape or sellotape). Finally, place a drawing pin in each corner. The paper will dry taut and flat and should not buckle when paint is applied. Occasionally, however, stretching does go wrong and the paper buckles at one corner or tears away from the gumstrip; if that happens there is no other course but to repeat the process. Drying can be hastened with a hair-drier, but it is not a good practice to leave the board in front of a fire. Ideally the paper should dry naturally.

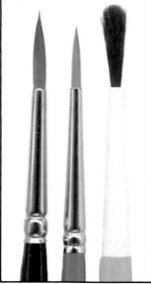

The differences between a quality sable brush (left), or synthetic sable (middle), and the kind of cheap brush sometimes provided in watercolour boxes (right), are self-evident.

◆ BRUSHES ◆

Soft brushes are normally used for watercolour. The best ones are sable, made from the tips of the tail hairs of the small rodent found chiefly in Siberia. Sable brushes are extremely expensive, but if looked after properly they should last a lifetime. Watercolour brushes are also made from squirrel-hair (known as 'camel hair' for some reason) and ox-hair. These are good substitutes for sable, but have less spring. There is now a wide range of synthetic brushes, usually made of nylon or a mixture of nylon and sable, and although they do not hold the paint as well as sable and are thus less suitable for broad washes, they are excellent for finer details and are very much chaper.

Brushes come in a variety of shapes and only by experiment will an individual discover which shapes and sizes suit him. It is not necessary to have a great many brushes for watercolour work; for most purposes three or four will be adequate, and many artists use only two. A practical range would be one large chisel-end for laying washes and two or three rounds in different sizes. Some watercolourists use ordinary household brushes for washes, but care must be taken to prevent hairs from falling out as you work.

If you want your brushes to last, it is essential to look

BELOW Soft sable brushes are the best brushes, but they are very expensive and many synthetic and sable and synthetic mixtures are now available. A beginner should not need more than one flat brush and two or three rounds; specialized brushes such as blenders and fans are used for particular techniques.

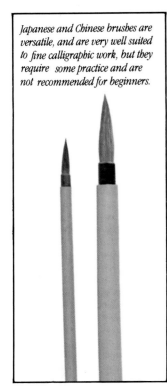

Japanese and Chinese brushes are versatile, and are very well suited to fine calligraphic work, but they require some practice and are not recommended for beginners.

LEFT *The complete range of sizes available of one make of brush.*

BELOW *A range of brush types used for particular techniques. From left to right: fine synthetic round, broad synthetic round, mixed fibres round, ox hair round, squirrel hair round, sable fan, sable bright, sable round, fine sable round.*

after them well. Wash them thoroughly in running water after use — if they are still stained use a little soap. Never leave brushes pointing downwards in a glass of water, as this will bend the hairs out of shape, possibly permanently. If they need to be stored for a length of time in a box or tin make sure that they are absolutely dry; otherwise mildew may form. Store them upright if possible.

A combined satchel and stool can make life easier when painting out of doors.

◆ EASELS ◆

Watercolours, unlike oils, are best done at close quarters, with the support held nearly horizontal, so that an easel is not really necessary for indoor work. However, an easel can be helpful. It allows you to tilt the work at different angles (many artists prefer to do preliminary drawings with the board held vertical) and to move it around to the best light, which is more difficult with a table. The most important aspects to consider — apart, of course, from price — are stability and the facility for holding the work firmly in a horizontal position. For outdoor work, the combined seat and easel, which folds and is carried by a handle, is particularly useful. For indoor work, the combination easel, which can be used both as a drawing table and a studio easel, is more convenient. Both are adjustable to any angle from vertical to horizontal. Good easels are not cheap, however, so that it is wise to do without one until you are sure of your requirements; many professional watercolourists work at an ordinary table with their board supported by a book or brick.

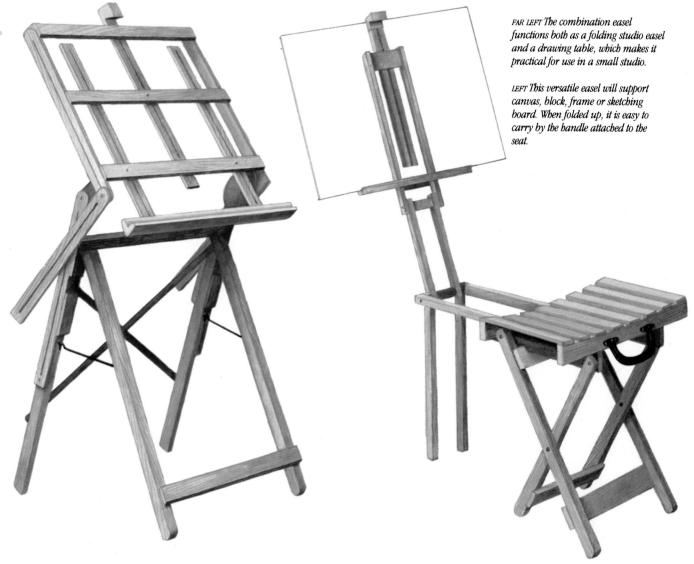

FAR LEFT The combination easel functions both as a folding studio easel and a drawing table, which makes it practical for use in a small studio.

LEFT This versatile easel will support canvas, block, frame or sketching board. When folded up, it is easy to carry by the handle attached to the seat.

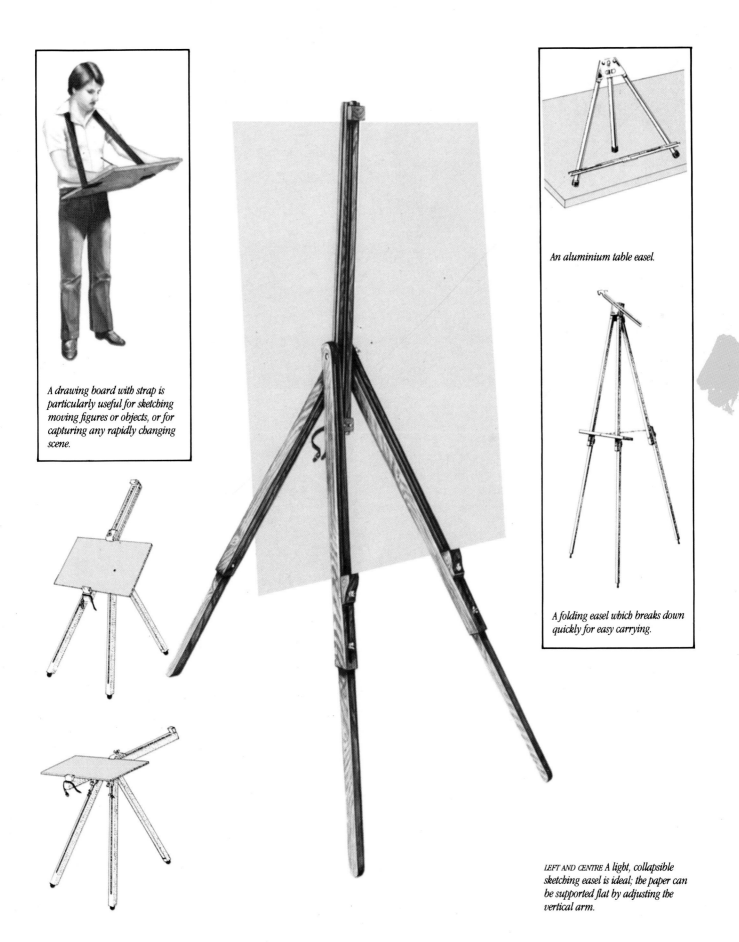

A drawing board with strap is particularly useful for sketching moving figures or objects, or for capturing any rapidly changing scene.

An aluminium table easel.

A folding easel which breaks down quickly for easy carrying.

LEFT AND CENTRE A light, collapsible sketching easel is ideal; the paper can be supported flat by adjusting the vertical arm.

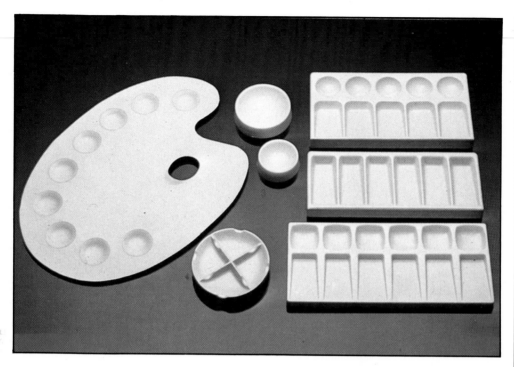

ABOVE Any plate or dish can be used for mixing watercolour, but there are several specially made palettes on the market. The thumbhole variety is especially useful for outdoor work.

These colours will provide a perfectly adequate range for most needs. Some artists work with fewer. From top to bottom: cobalt blue, Prussian blue, viridian, yellow ochre, cadmium yellow, lemon yellow, cadmium red, alizarin crimson, burnt umber, Payne's grey and ivory black.

◆ LIGHTING ◆

For indoor work it is vital to organize a good system of lighting. Working by a window with light coming over your left shoulder (or right shoulder if you are left-handed) can be quite satisfactory if the window faces north and gives an even and relatively unchanging light. It is less so if the window faces the sun, since the light may constantly change from brilliant to murky and may even throw distracting patches of light and shade across your work. An artificial light of the fluorescent 'daylight' type will enable you to work in a poorly lit room or corner and to continue working when the light has faded — winter days can seem very short for those dependent on daylight. Such light can be used either instead of natural light or to supplement it, and there is one type with a screw base that can be fitted to the edge of a table or an adjacent shelf.

◆ BOARDS, PALETTES AND ◆ OTHER EQUIPMENT

You will need a drawing board, or possibly two boards of different sizes, to support the paper and stretch it where necessary. A piece of plywood or blockboard is perfectly adequate provided the surface is smooth and the wood soft enough to take drawing pins. For outdoor work a piece of hardboard can be used, with the paper clipped to it, though the paper must be heavy enough not to require stretching.

If you buy paints in paintbox form you will already have a palette; if not, you will need one with compartments for mixing paint. Watercolour palettes are made in plastic, metal or ceramic, in a variety of sizes, and some have a thumbhole so that they can be held in the non-painting

Small natural sponges are an invaluable aid to watercolour painting, both for applying paint and for correcting or modifying areas. Rags, kitchen paper and cotton buds should also form part of the basic equipment.

hand when working out of doors. Water containers are another necessity for outdoor work; there is nothing worse than arriving at your chosen spot to find that you have forgotten the water. Containers can be bought, plastic soft-drink bottles can be used to carry the water and any light (unbreakable) container such as a yogurt pot will suffice to put it in.

Various other items, though not strictly essential, can be useful and inexpensive aids for watercolour work. Small sponges can be used instead of brushes to apply washes, to sponge out areas and to create soft, smudgy cloud effects; kitchen roll, blotting paper and cotton wool can be used in much the same way. Toothbrushes are useful for spattering paint to create textured effects, to suggest sand or pebbles on a beach, for example. A scalpel, or a razor blade, is often used to scrape away small areas of paint in a highlight area. And both masking tape and masking fluid can serve to stop out areas while a wash is laid over the top, leaving a hard-edged area of white paper when removed. The specific uses of such aids and devices are more fully explained in the following chapter, and examples are given in the step-by-step demonstrations in the latter part of the book.

CHAPTER THREE

TECHNIQUE

*A detail from a painting of a French vineyard: the artist
decided that the converging lines of the field were too heavily
coloured. He loosens the colour with a soft brush and clean
water, before lifting it off with tissue.*

*P*URE WATERCOLOUR, being transparent, must be applied from light to dark. The paper itself is used to create the pure white or light tones which, with opaque paints, would be made by using white alone or mixed with coloured pigment.

Any area required to be white is simply 'reserved', or left unpainted, so that when it is surrounded with darker washes it will shine out with great brilliance. Pale tones are created in the same way, with a light-coloured wash put on first and then surrounded with darker tones. Light reflected off the paper, back through these thin skins of paint known as washes, gives a watercolour painting a spontaneity and sparkle which cannot be achieved with any other medium. Hence watercolour's popularity with artists both past and present.

The two most important facts about watercolour are, first, that it is always to some extent unpredictable, even in the hands of experts, and, second, that because dark is always worked over light, some planning is needed before beginning the painting. It is not always necessary to do a detailed and complicated drawing on the paper, only enough to work out the basic shapes and design; this really should be done however, or you will begin without really knowing which areas are to be left white or pale and how they will fit into the painting as a whole.

Thus the first step in any painting is to establish where the first wash is to be applied; and the first step in watercolour technique is to learn how to put on the wash.

♦ LAYING A FLAT WASH ♦

The wash is the basis of all watercolour painting, whether it is a broad, sweeping one, covering a large expanse, such as a sky or the background to a portrait, or a much smaller one laid on a particular area. Washes need not be totally flat. They can be gradated in both tone and colour, or broken up and varied. But the technique of laying a flat wash must be mastered, even if you subsequently find that you seldom use it.

The support should be tilted at a slight angle so that the brush strokes flow into one another, but do not run down the paper. For a broad wash a large chisel-end brush is normally used; for a smaller one, or a wash which is to be laid against a complicated edge, a smaller round brush may be more manageable. Laying a wash must be done quickly or hard edges will form between brush strokes. Therefore mix up more paint than you think you will need. Start by damping the paper with clear water (this is not actually essential, but helps the paint to go on evenly). Working in one direction, lay a horizontal line of colour at the top of the area, then another below it, working in the opposite direction, and continue working in alternate directions until the area is covered. Never go back over the wet paint because you feel it is uneven or not dark enough, as this will result in the paint's 'flooding' and leave blobs and patches. A final word of caution: if the doorbell or the

FLAT WASH.

A flat wash in a vivid colour is being laid on dampened paper with a broad, flat-ended brush. It is not strictly necessary to dampen the paper (many artists prefer the slightly 'dragged' look given by working on dry paper) but dampening facilitates an even covering. Tilt the board slightly so that the brush strokes flow into one another, and work backwards and forwards down the paper until the whole area is covered.

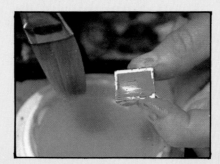

SPONGE WASH.

Often a wash needs to be slightly textured or varied in strength, for which purpose a sponge is useful.
1. *The wash is mixed with a brush and tested on a piece of spare paper.*

2. *Enough paint is mixed to cover the area and the sponge is dipped into it. For a lighter covering, some of the paint can be squeezed out.*

3. *A variegated effect is achieved by applying the paint quite thickly with the first stroke, much more thinly with the second.*

4. *The final wash can be worked into with the sponge while it is still wet in order to lighten some areas and produce a soft, shimmering effect.*

VARIEGATED WASH.

1. *The paper is dampened with a sponge and a thin wash of colour is applied, also with a sponge.*

2. *A second colour is then flooded on, using the tip of the sponge so that the two run together.*

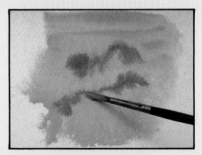

3. *A brush is now used to touch in darker areas on the still-wet paint. Very subtle effects can be created by this wet-into-wet technique, but they are always to some extent unpredictable.*

telephone rings while you are in the middle of a wash, ignore it; otherwise you will return to a hard edge which is impossible, or at least very difficult to remove.

Leave the wash to dry before working on adjacent areas of the painting. Not until the wash is completely dry will you be able to establish either how even it is or what its true colour value is (watercolour dries much paler than it appears when wet). The ability to assess the precise tone of a wash comes only with experience, but it can be helpful to lay down one or two patches of flat colour on a spare piece of paper and allow them to dry as a preliminary test. Washes can be laid on top of the first one to strengthen the colour or darken the tone, though too many will turn the painting muddy. Purists claim that more than three layers spoils the quality.

Another method of laying a wash is to use a sponge. This is particularly useful when a slightly variegated or textured wash is required, as the sponge can either be filled with paint for a dense covering or used relatively dry for a paler effect. A sponge can also be used in conjunction with a brush. If, for instance, you rinse it in clean water and squeeze it out you can remove some of the paint laid by a brush while it is still wet, thus lightening selected areas — a good technique for skies or distant hills.

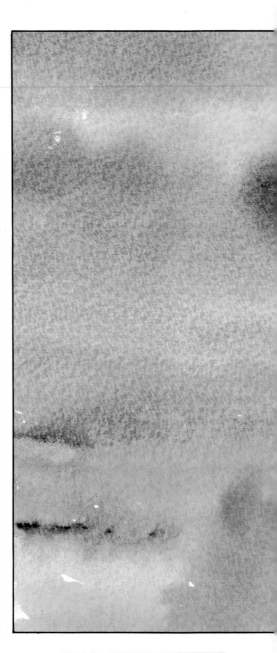

◆ COMPLEX EDGES ◆

Sometimes a wash must be laid against a complicated edge, for example, a group of roofs and chimneys with an intricate outline. The wash must then start from the edge rather than end at it, which may necessitate turning the board sideways or upside down. When dampening the paper before putting on the wash take care to dampen only up to this edge; otherwise the wash will flow into the areas to be reserved.

This kind of technical problem highlights the need for initial planning — the success of a painting may hinge on the precise way a certain area has been outlined by reserving. Another method for dealing with intricate shapes is to stop out the parts to be reserved with masking fluid.

◆ GRADATED AND VARIEGATED ◆ WASHES

Colours in nature are seldom totally flat or one solid hue. It is often desirable, therefore, to lay a gradated wash, which becomes darker or lighter at the top or bottom or changes from one colour to another. For a gradated wash, simply mix more water with the paint to make each successive strip lighter or more pigment to darken them.

For a variegated wash, mix up the two or more colours to be used, dampen the paper as usual, and then lay on the colours so that they blend into one another. The effect of such a wash cannot be worked out precisely in advance, even with practice — you should be prepared for a happy (or unhappy) accident. As with a flat wash, never make corrections while the paint is still wet; if you are dissatis-

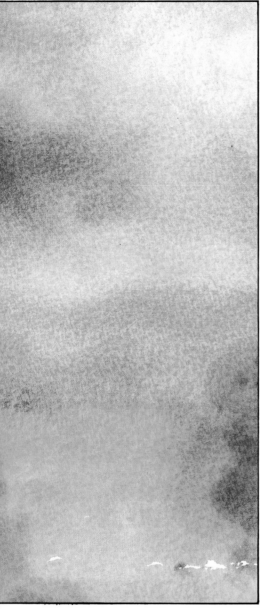

DRY-BRUSH.

Dry-brush work is an excellent method of suggesting texture, such as that of grass or a corn field, but it becomes monotonous if used too much in one painting. Here a number of similar colours have been used over a pale underlying wash to give tonal variation.

FAR LEFT Prussian blue and alizarin crimson have been allowed to run into one another, just as they would with a wash of only one colour. Such effects are impossible to control accurately; the artist must be prepared for an element of 'happy accident'.

MIDDLE Laying one wash on top of another often gives textural variety as well as intensifying the colour. Notice that the bottom band, a pale wash of Payne's grey, is quite even, while the one at the top, a third application of the same wash, shows distinct brush marks.

ABOVE The possibilities of working wet into wet may be explored by producing this kind of doodle in a matter of minutes. The wet-into-wet technique is often used in the early stages of a painting, or for the background, more precise work being done at a later stage or in another area of the painting.

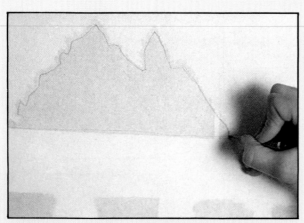

1. *The artist uses detail paper to trace the area he wants to mask.*

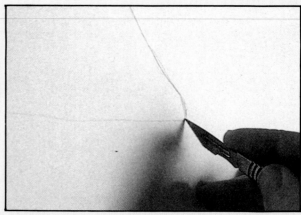

2. *He then carefully cuts the mask with a scalpel.*

4. *More sap green, again mixed with gum water, is spattered on the area with an ordinary household brush.*

5. *The slightly irregular stippled effect is clear, even before the mask is peeled off.*

fied when it is dry it can be sponged out and a further wash laid on top.

Some watercolourists use variegated washes in a particularly free way. Each individual arrives at his own technique by trial and error. Attractive efforts can sometimes be achieved by deliberately allowing the paint to flood in the middle of a wash, by introducing blobs of strong colour to a paler wash while the paint is damp, or by laying one wash over a dry one, thus producing a slight granulation of the paper. Such effects are unpredictable. For one thing, they vary widely according to the type of paper used. But one of the great joys of watercolour is the opportunity it provides for turning accidental effects to advantage.

♦ DRY-BRUSH AND TEXTURAL ♦ METHODS

Painting with a small amount of paint on a fine brush which is almost dry is a method most frequently used for the fine details of a painting, but dry-brush is also a technique in its own right and can be used very effectively for large areas, either over a wash which has already been laid down or straight on to white paper. For landscape work it can be used to suggest the texture of grass, trees, rocks, stone walls and the like. For portraits and still-lifes it can model forms more easily than washes of wet paint can.

Like all watercolour techniques dry-brush requires practice. If the paint is too wet it will go on as a solid wash; if too dry it will not go on at all. The brush normally used for large areas of dry-brush work is a large chisel-end, with the bristles slightly splayed to produce a series of fine lines, rather like hatching and cross-hatching in drawing. One colour and tone can be laid over another, and the brush strokes can be put on in different directions as the shape suggests.

The Victorian artist, William Holman Hunt (1827-1910) used this method extensively, together with stippling, in which small dots of colour are applied to the paper very close together, in rather the way that the

3. *The mask is applied and the tree is painted in sap green, mixed with a little gum water to give it extra body and brilliance.*

6. *The mask is removed, leaving a sharp, clean outline. The slightly irregular texture is very effective in suggesting foliage.*

USING MASKING FLUID.

Masking fluid provides a way of painting in 'negative', which can give very subtle and exciting effects.

1. *The areas to be masked are carefully drawn and the fluid is applied with a fine brush.*

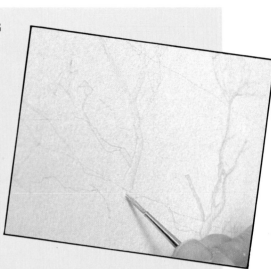

2. *The fluid is allowed to dry and a yellow-brown wash is laid over the top.*

3. *A blue wash for the sky is added and allowed to dry, after which the fluid is peeled off by gentle rubbing with a finger.*

French artist, Georges Seurat (1859-91), applied oil paint.

Scumbling is a method of applying fairly thick paint in a circular scrubbing motion so that the paint goes on to the paper from all directions and picks up the texture of the surface. It is effective when used for relatively small areas to provide contrast to flat washes, but if used too extensively in one painting it can become monotonous.

Another common method of suggesting texture is to spatter wet paint on to the paper with a toothbrush or bristle-brush. This technique, too, should be reserved for certain areas only, but it is an excellent way of dealing with a pebble beach, say, or a rough stone wall. The paint is usually spattered over an existing wash not directly on to white paper, and to make the result look natural care must be taken to use paint which is not much darker than the wash. Mask off surrounding areas if they are lighter in tone.

Masking tape can be used for a straight edge; for more complex shapes, a rough mask can be cut from cartridge paper.

♦ MASKING OUT AND CREATING ♦ HIGHLIGHTS

Many watercolourists use masking fluid and masking tape for reserving areas of white paper. Masking fluid, which is specially made for the purpose, is a kind of liquid rubber sold in small bottles and applied with a brush. Purists disdain to use it, but their scorn is baseless. Very attractive and exciting effects, quite different from those produced by the classic method of laying washes around an area, can be gained by it. Stopping out with masking fluid is a method of painting in 'negative'; the precise and subtle shades made by the brush remain when the liquid is removed.

The paper must be quite dry before the fluid is applied, and the fluid itself must be allowed to dry before a wash is laid on top. Once the wash has dried, the fluid can be rubbed off with a finger or a soft eraser, leaving the white area, which can be modified and worked into if required. Masking fluid should never be left on the paper for longer than necessary, and care must be taken to wash the brushes immediately; otherwise fluid will harden in the hairs and ruin them. Masking fluid is not suitable for all papers, especially ones with a rough surface.

Masking tape is particularly useful for straight-edged areas, such as the light-catching side of a building or the edge of a window-sill. There is no reason why all painting should be done freehand; just as few people can draw a circle without recourse to compasses, few people can paint a really straight line without splashing paint over the edge. Masking tape enables you to use the paint freely without worrying about spoiling the area to be reserved.

Yet another way of keeping the paint away from the paper is to use wax in what is called the resist method, like that used in batik fabrics. This differs from the previous techniques in being permanent; once the wax is on the paper it cannot be removed except by laborious scraping with a razor blade. The paint, moreover, will lie on top of the wax to some extent (this varies according to the paper used), leaving a slightly textured surface. The effect can be very attractive, particularly for flowers or fabrics. An ordinary household candle can be used, or a white wax crayon for finer lines.

The best method of creating fine, delicate highlights when a painting is nearly complete is to scrape into the paint with a sharp point, of a scalpel, say, so that the white paper is revealed. Very fine lines can be drawn in this way to suggest a blade of grass or a flower stem catching the light in the foreground of a landscape. Such touches often give a painting that extra something it seems to need. They can also be achieved by applying Chinese white with a fine brush, but scraping back tends to give a cleaner line.

♦ MIXING MEDIA ♦

Many other media can be used in combination with watercolour; indeed, the mixing of media is now commonplace, whereas in the past it was regarded as

ABOVE *Watercolour has been used in conjunction with pastel to give liveliness and textural contrast to this painting. Both the building itself and the dark tree on the left are in pure watercolour, while the foreground grass is pure pastel. The sky is a combination of the two. Pastel combines well with watercolour, and a painting such as this often benefits from a 'non-purist' approach.*

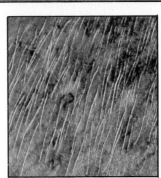

LEFT Sharp, clean lines and highlights can be made by scraping into dry paint with a scalpel or other sharp knife. Take care not to damage the paper by pressing too hard.

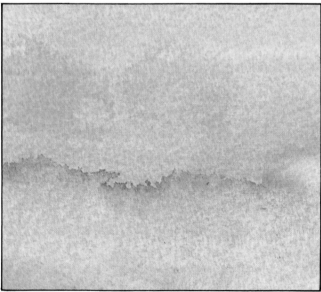

*A wash which has 'gone wrong'
ABOVE and flooded, has been worked
into to create a sky effect not
originally planned TOP. One of the
attractions of watercolour is that
new uses of the medium are often
supported by 'mistakes'.*

breaking the rules. Watercolour used with pen and ink has a long history; in the days before watercolour became recognized as a medium in its own right, it was used mainly to give touches of colour to drawings or to tint black and white engravings. Nowadays there are many other media — some old and some new — that can be used with watercolour to good effect.

One traditional way to change the nature of paint by thickening it is to mix it with a little gum arabic, which gives it both texture and lasting lustre. Soap can be used in much the same way, and it makes the paint easier to scrape back. Soap can also be used to make imprints of objects such as leaves or flowers. Coat the object with soap, apply paint to it and then press it on to the paper.

Watercolours can be drawn into with pens, pencils, crayons or pastels, and areas can be stressed or lightened with gouache or Chinese white. Watercolour pencils and crayons, a relatively new invention, are particularly suitable for this purpose. When dry they behave like crayons or hard pastels, but if dipped in water or used on wet paper they will dissolve, forming a wash. Using these, or ordinary pastels, on top of watercolour can turn a painting which has 'gone wrong' and become dull and lifeless into something quite new and different. It is always worth experimenting with such media on a painting that you are less than happy with; you may evolve a personal technique that you can use again. Wax oil pastels can create interesting textured areas when laid underneath a wash, as can treating the paper, or parts of it, with white spirit before painting, which has a similar effect. The possibilities are almost endless, and experimentation is sure to reward you with interesting discoveries.

◆ PROBLEM-SOLVING ◆

Although watercolours cannot be altered so drastically or so often as paintings in any of the opaque media, changes are possible. It is a mistake to abandon a picture because a first wash has not gone on quite right.

The first thing to remember is that a wash which looks too dark or too vivid on a sheet of otherwise white paper will dry much lighter and may look quite pale when surrounded by other colours. If the first wash looks wrong, let it dry. If you are still quite sure it is not what you intended, sponge it out with a clean sponge and clear water. This may leave a slight stain on the paper, depending on the paper used and the colour itself (some colours stain the paper, like a dye, while others do not) but when dry it will be too faint to spoil the new wash. When a wash has flooded, sponge it out immediately without waiting for it to dry; flooding cannot be entirely remedied, though it can sometimes create an effect not originally planned.

One of the commonest faults is accidentally to take a wash over the edge of an area to be reserved. There are three ways of dealing with this, depending on the size of the area and the type of edge desired. If the wash is pale and the area to be reserved is a broad and imprecise shape, such as a stone in the foreground of a landscape, you can simply sponge out the excess paint with a small sponge or cotton wool damped in clean water. A soft edge will be left. For a more intricate shape, or one requiring a sharp, clear edge, you may have to scrape the paint away (after it is dry) with a razor blade or scalpel, the former for broad areas, the latter for small ones. Hold the blade flat on the paper so that the corners do not dig in and scrape gently. The same method can be used to lighten an area or to create texture by removing a top layer of paint. The third rescue technique — to apply Chinese white with a fine brush — should be used only when the painting is otherwise complete; if the white is allowed to mix with other colours it will muddy them and spoil the translucency.

The small blots and smudges that often occur when you take a loaded brush over a painting or rest your hand on a still-damp area can also be razored out when dry. If a splash of paint or dirty water falls on the painting, quickly soak up the excess with a twist of tissue or a cotton bud, let it dry and then razor it out gently. If you are intending to apply more paint to the area, rub it down lightly with a soft eraser to smooth the surface, which will have been slightly roughened.

Even professionals, of course, sometimes find that a painting has gone so wrong that small corrections will not suffice or has become so clogged with paint that further work is impossible. If this happens you can, of course, throw it away. But you can also wash out the whole painting, or large parts of it, by putting the paper under running water and sponging the surface. Leave it on its board if you have stretched it. A slight stain may be left, but this can be an advantage as the faint shadow will serve as a drawing for the next attempt. A whole sky or foreground can be removed in this way, while leaving intact those areas with which you are satisfied.

USING GUM WATER.

Gum water, which is gum arabic diluted in water, adds richness to watercolours and keeps the colours bright. It can also be used, as here, as a sort of resist method to create highlights.
1. The tree and hedge are painted in with pure watercolour.
2. A further wash of green is applied, this time mixed with gum water.
3. The area of the central tree is spattered with water, flicked on with a household brush.
4. The central tree is blotted with a rag, so that wherever the water has touched, small areas of paint are lifted off, the gum being soluble in water.
5. The lighter patches of colour give an extra sparkle to the tree, while the addition of the gum water imparts richness to the dark green on either side.

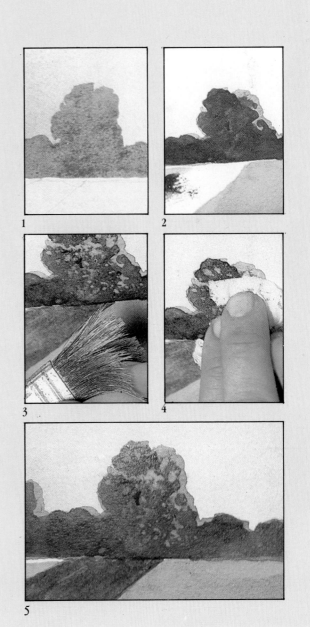

CHAPTER FOUR

BASIC RULES FOR ARTISTS

Working outdoors. Some artists find that they work best with the subject in front of them. Others will only work from sketches or photographs, or even (more rarely), from memory.

*E*VERY PAINTER, working in whatever medium, needs to understand the basic rules of his craft, even if sometimes only to break them. The underlying principles of such things as composition, perspective, drawing itself, apply to all kinds of painting. The novice watercolourist, who needs to plan his paintings especially carefully, should have a firm grasp of them from the beginning.

♦ COMPOSING AND SELECTING ♦

Whether you are painting outdoors or indoors, whether your chosen subject is a landscape, a group of buildings, a portrait or a single flower in a vase, you need to have a clear idea of what the main elements are and of how you will place them on the paper before you begin to paint. Painting a landscape out of doors requires you to decide where the view is to begin and end, where to place the horizon, whether to emphasize or alter features in the foreground, and so on. For a portrait, still-life or flower painting you must decide how much to show, the proportion of the figure or flower in relation to the background, the general colour scheme and the balance of lights and darks. Composition and selection thus go hand in hand: an artist first selects which aspects of the subject are important and then composes the picture by placing them in a certain way.

There are well-tested mathematical rules for 'good composition'. The ancient Greeks, for instance, devised the system known as the Golden Section (or Golden Mean), in which the area of the painting is divided by a line in such a way that the smaller part is to the larger what the larger is to the whole. This ensures that the picture plane is divided in a balanced and symmetrical way, and countless artists have made use of the principle. The triangle is another basis for composition (many paintings are based on the framework of a single triangle) as is a series of intersecting geometric shapes such as squares, rectangles and circles.

It is unlikely that someone sitting down to an outdoor watercolour sketch will need a full knowledge of such principles, but there are some simple and practical ones that should be borne in mind. Basically, a good composi-

ABOVE *Figure paintings are more difficult to compose than landscapes because the choices are so much wider. A figure can be disposed in an almost infinite number of ways, while a landscape often needs only minor re-arranging. Here the artist has placed his subject in the centre of the picture, with the diagonal of the leg balancing the angle of the head. He has allowed one leg and the legs of the chair to 'bust' the frame at the bottom, thus bringing the figure forward on to the picture plane and avoiding a cramped and awkward appearance.*

Painters of the Renaissance usually planned the composition of a painting on a geometric grid structure. This example, by Piero della Francesca, is based on a triangle, a common compositional device which is still much used, as are circles and rectangles. The drawing on the right shows how other triangles can be discerned within the main one formed by the figures.

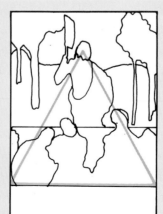

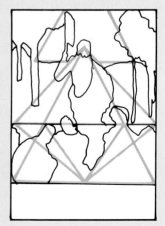

LEFT Converging lines in landscapes are often used to lead the viewer's eye to the focal point, in this case the buildings. Unusually, the artist has divided the picture into two nearly equal parts, the land and the sky; but monotony has been avoided by allowing the buildings and trees to break into the skyline and by dividing the foreground by the broken line of white road in the middle distance.

tion is one in which there are no jarring elements; all the parts of the picture balance one another in a pleasing way, and the viewer's eye is led into the picture rather than out of it. Whatever the subject, it is almost never advisable to divide the painting into two equal halves, such as sea and land, or table-top and background in a still-life. The result is at once monotonous and disjointed. The viewer's eye should not be led to one part of the painting to the exclusion of others, but there should usually be a 'focal point'. For example, a group of buildings in a landscape can be used simply as a counterpoint to other elements, such as trees and hills, or they may be what interests you most about the scene, with the trees, hills and foreground used as a 'backdrop'. The buildings need not be large, nor placed directly in the centre of the picture (this is not normally advisable); what matters is that the eye should be consistently led to them as the focal point. Compositional devices often used to lead the eye in this way are the curving lines of a path, stream, ploughed field or fence, along which the viewer's eye must travel. Such lines should never lead out of the picture unless for a deliberately sought effect.

The focal point of a portrait is almost always the face, the eyes in particular for a front or three-quarter view, and care must be taken not to detract from it by placing too much emphasis on other elements, such as the background, or the hands. Hands and clothing are often treated in a sketchy way so that they do not assume too much importance. A figure or face should be placed in a well-considered and deliberate way against the background to create a feeling of harmony and balance. There should not be too much space at the top. Nor, usually, should the subject be placed squarely in the middle of the picture, though a central position can sometimes be effective.

Backgrounds are part of a portrait painting, as are skies in landscapes, even when they are quite plain and muted in colour. If a picture is placed against a stark white background, the white areas will have their own shapes

and thus make their contribution to the balance of the painting. Such flat areas are known as 'negative space'. A more decorative background, such as a boldly patterned wallpaper or still-life of a vase of flowers on a table, can be used to complement the main subject, just as the colours in the sky or the direction of clouds do in a landscape.

Many artists use viewing frames to help them work out a satisfactory composition, and some also use polaroid cameras for indoor work, taking several shots of a portrait or still-life until they find a satisfactory arrangement. A viewing frame is simply a piece of cardboard with an oblong hole cut in it (a good size of aperture is 4½ × 6 in /11 × 15 cm), which is held up at about arm's length to

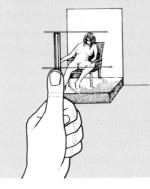

When drawing a figure from life measurements and angles need constant checking. By holding up a pencil and moving your thumb up and down on it you can check proportions; angling the pencil to follow the line of the body or limb shows you the precise slope, which can be double-checked by relating it to a vertical, such as a chair leg.

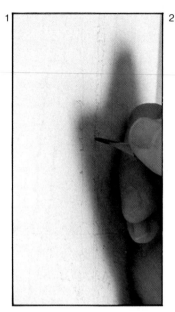

LEFT This study of a motel required a careful outline drawing to enable the artist to place his first wash accurately.

TOP RIGHT AND ABOVE Since only an outline was needed, the drawing was done directly on the support with a sharp 2B pencil. The first wash was then laid around the shapes of the building and trees.

is quite dry. On most papers pencil marks can be erased without affecting the paint on top, though the surface of a few, rather smooth, papers may be spoiled by too much erasing.

◆ PERSPECTIVE ◆

Perspective is sometimes believed to be the concern only of those who paint buildings. In fact, the laws of perspective govern everything, simply because drawing and painting transfer three-dimensional shapes on to a two-dimensional surface.

In theory, a perfectly adequate drawing with a fairly accurate rendering of perspective could be produced by simply drawing what is seen. Some knowledge of the basic principles of perspective is nevertheless helpful, if only

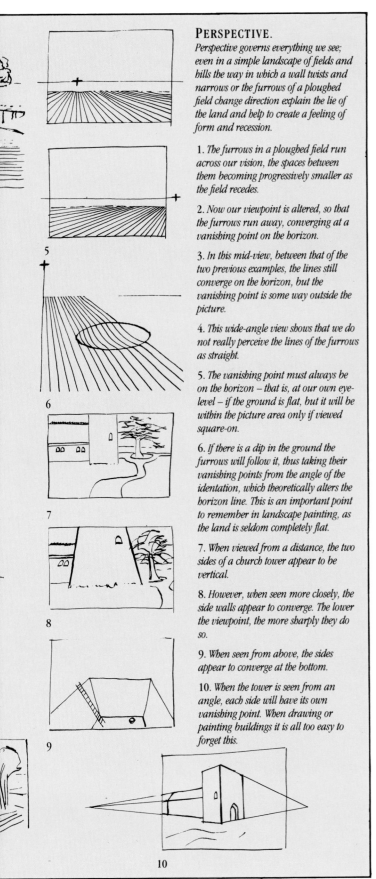

PERSPECTIVE.

Perspective governs everything we see; even in a simple landscape of fields and hills the way in which a wall twists and narrows or the furrows of a ploughed field change direction explain the lie of the land and help to create a feeling of form and recession.

1. The furrows in a ploughed field run across our vision, the spaces between them becoming progressively smaller as the field recedes.

2. Now our viewpoint is altered, so that the furrows run away, converging at a vanishing point on the horizon.

3. In this mid-view, between that of the two previous examples, the lines still converge on the horizon, but the vanishing point is some way outside the picture.

4. This wide-angle view shows that we do not really perceive the lines of the furrows as straight.

5. The vanishing point must always be on the horizon – that is, at our own eye-level – if the ground is flat, but it will be within the picture area only if viewed square-on.

6. If there is a dip in the ground the furrows will follow it, thus taking their vanishing points from the angle of the identation, which theoretically alters the horizon line. This is an important point to remember in landscape painting, as the land is seldom completely flat.

7. When viewed from a distance, the two sides of a church tower appear to be vertical.

8. However, when seen more closely, the side walls appear to converge. The lower the viewpoint, the more sharply they do so.

9. When seen from above, the sides appear to converge at the bottom.

10. When the tower is seen from an angle, each side will have its own vanishing point. When drawing or painting buildings it is all too easy to forget this.

because it will enable you to know when something has gone wrong. The 'golden rule', which most people learn at school, is that receding parallel lines meet at a vanishing point. That vanishing point, which is on the horizon, may be inside the picture area or outside it. The horizon itself is your own eye-level, so that if you are lying down or crouching it will be low, with a large expanse of sky, whereas if you are looking down on a scene, from a top-floor window, say, it will be very high, perhaps with no sky visible at all, and a receding parallel line of rooftops below you will slope upwards. The real difficulty in drawing complex perspective subjects, such as urban scenes, is that buildings have several different planes, each with its own vanishing point, and sometimes one building or group of buildings is set at angles to another, giving yet another set of points, many of which will be outside the picture plane. These must be guessed at to some extent, but the pencil-and-thumb measuring system described earlier is helpful, or a small plastic ruler can be held up to assess the angles of parallel lines.

Artists frequently distort perspective intentionally, or use it in an inventive way by choosing an artificially high or low viewpoint. Others ignore it altogether, to create paintings with a strong pattern, rather as children do. There is no reason why the rules should not be broken if doing so makes a better painting. But to break rules successfully it is necessary first to understand them.

◆ TONE AND COLOUR ◆

Colour theory can be enormously complicated. It is a fascinating study in itself, about which whole books have been written. But there are really only a few facts about colour which the average painter needs to know. Colour has two main components, tone and hue, the former being its lightness or darkness and the latter its intensity, or vividness. If you were to take both a black-and-white photograph and a colour one of a landscape composed almost entirely of greens, the black-and-white one would show the tones quite clearly as a series of dark greys and light greys shading to white and black. It is important to balance tones, or lights and darks, in a painting, but they can be rather hard to assess, particularly outdoors in a changing light. You may wonder whether the sky is lighter or darker than the sea or land, or whether the leaves of a tree are lighter or darker than the hills behind. Tones are much easier to judge if you half-close your eyes, thus eliminating distracting details.

In the colour photograph of the landscape some of the greens will appear more vivid than others, to have a brighter hue. You may notice that the brightest colours are in the foreground, where the contrasts in tone are also the strongest, those in the background tending to merge into one another and become barely distinguishable in places. An understanding of this phenomenon, called aerial perspective, is vitally important, especially for the land-scape painter. As a landscape recedes into the middle and then the far distance, objects appear much less distinct and become paler and bluer because the light is filtered

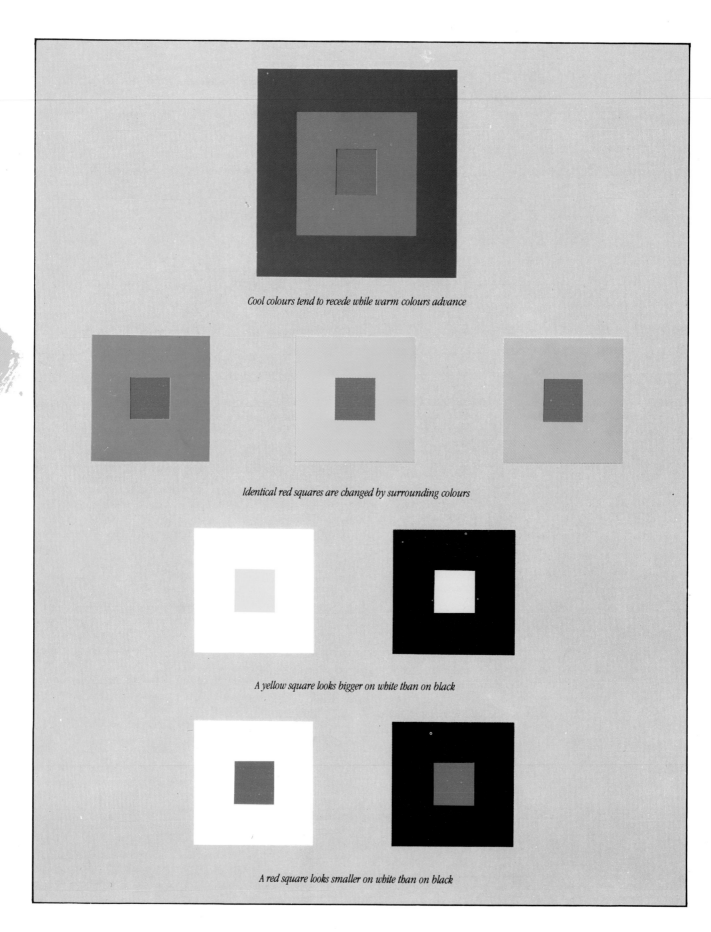

Cool colours tend to recede while warm colours advance

Identical red squares are changed by surrounding colours

A yellow square looks bigger on white than on black

A red square looks smaller on white than on black

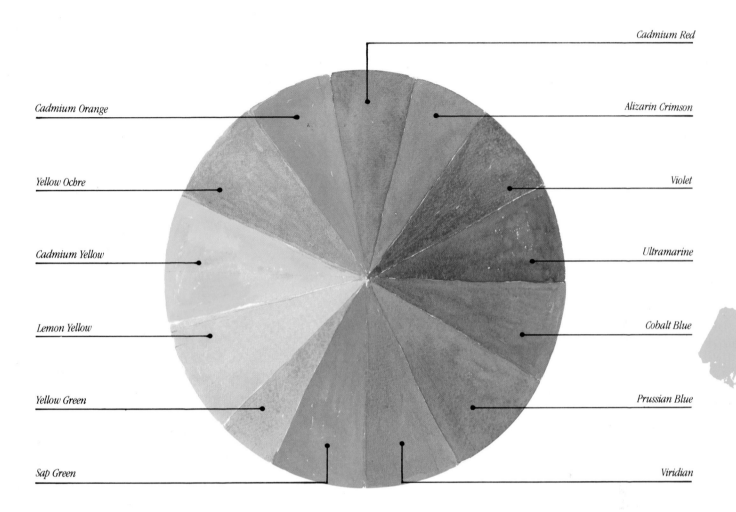

Cadmium Red

Cadmium Orange

Alizarin Crimson

Yellow Ochre

Violet

Cadmium Yellow

Ultramarine

Lemon Yellow

Cobalt Blue

Yellow Green

Prussian Blue

Sap Green

Viridian

LEFT The single most important fact to realize about colour is that each colour exists only in relation to those surrounding it. Not only does the relative 'temperature' of a colour, that is, its warmness or coolness change, but the apparent size of an area of colour also changes according to its surroundings. These are examples of optical illusions produced by such juxtapositions.

through dust and moisture in the atmosphere. It is possible to suggest distance and recession in a painting by using this kind of perspective alone, and such effects are easier to achieve in watercolour than in oil: a pale, flat wash can be put on and then the tiny differences in tones suggested by just a dab or two of barely tinted water.

Colours in the foreground tend to be 'warmer' than those in the background as well as brighter in hue. All colours can be broadly classified as either 'warm' or 'cool'. Reds, yellows and oranges, for instance, are warm, and tend to push themselves forward, or 'advance'; blues, and colours with blue in them, such as blue-grey and blue-green, will recede. However, colours can be perceived as colours only in relation to one another, and some blues are warmer than others while some reds are cooler. You can see this by placing ultramarine blue, which is relatively warm, next to the cold Prussian blue, or alizarin crimson, which is quite cool, next to cadmium red or orange, both of which are very warm.

Another way of using colour effectively is to make use of complementary colours, those that are opposite one another on the colour wheel. Red and green are complementaries, as are blue and yellow. A large expanse of green grass or blue sea can often be heightened by a small patch of bright red or yellow respectively. Landscape

ABOVE The colour wheel, which is really just a spectrum bent into a circle, is a useful device for working out combinations of colours. Notice how the colours on the red and yellow side appear warm, while those on the green and blue side are much cooler.

ABOVE *In this painting all the colours are cool, just a range of blues and greys with a touch of warmer greenish brown on the left side of the building. Foregrounds are often brought forward and emphasized by using warmer colours in the front of the picture; but here the foreground has been made to 'advance' by the use of much darker tones, aided by the very clear definition of the spiky foliage on the left.*

RIGHT *Warm colours have been used throughout this painting, those in the foreground being repeated in smaller quantities in the background. The artist's concern was with the pattern created by the various elements rather than with a strict three-dimensional representation, though the background recedes just enough to allow us to 'read' the picture as an urban landscape.*

and seascape painters often use a figure or the sail of a boat as a means of introducing a complementary colour.

Perhaps the single most important fact about colour is that there is no colour at all without light. The quality, strength and direction of the light changes colours constantly, a problem when working out of doors, as a landscape which might have seemed to be composed of tones of greenish grey in the morning could by evening have become golden ochre, even red, in places. The best ways to overcome the difficulty are to work quickly, possibly making several sketches under different lights, or to decide on a colour scheme and stick to it, ignoring subsequent changes. The problem is less acute when working indoors, though if natural light is being used for a portrait or still-life the colours will undoubtedly change, as will the way the shadows fall.

♦ USING REFERENCE MATERIAL ♦

Paintings do not, of course, have to be done from life: many fine landscapes are painted in the studio, and excellent portraits are done from photographs or drawings or a combination of both. Few good paintings, however, are done from memory. Even professional artists, who are trained to observe and assess and are constantly on the lookout for visual stimulus, make use of reference material for their paintings. These may be sketches or photographs, sometimes even picture postcards. You may think that you remember a scene very well, but you will be surprised how the details escape you as soon as you sit down to paint it. It is therefore wise to amass as much reference material as possible, even if it seems to be much more than you need.

Carrying a sketchbook is recommended — if nothing else it encourages the analytical observation of things, which is quite different from just looking and admiring. The trouble with sketches is that it takes experience to know which particular aspect or detail of a scene you will want to refer to later. Also, unless you draw with assurance, you may find that you have failed to capture the essence of what you wished to record — rather like taking notes and finding you cannot read your own shorthand or handwriting.

The camera is useful as a notetaker, but it should not be regarded as any more than this. Never try to copy a photograph slavishly. If you are out walking and see a promising subject, take several photographs, and when you begin the painting try to use them constructively, as a starting point, together with your own recollections of the scene, departing from both if you feel it would improve the painting. Portrait painters often have a preliminary live sitting and then photographs for later stages, or for the clothes and background.

The great advantage of photographs is that they can capture fleeting moments and impressions, such as the light falling in a certain way on a stretch of water, the eerie purple and gold light before a storm, children playing, or a cat asleep in a patch of sunlight. The disadvantage is that they do not actually tell the truth: the camera distorts perspective, flattens colour and fudges detail. When you want a clear visual description of some small, but vital, part of a subject, you find only a vague blur. A sketch, even a less than brilliant one, would probably have been more useful, because you would have been forced to look hard at the subject and thus have gained more understanding of it.

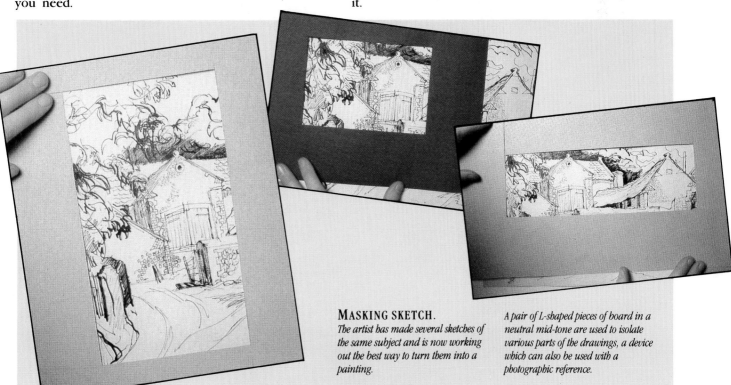

MASKING SKETCH.
The artist has made several sketches of the same subject and is now working out the best way to turn them into a painting.

A pair of L-shaped pieces of board in a neutral mid-tone are used to isolate various parts of the drawings, a device which can also be used with a photographic reference.

CHAPTER FIVE

LANDSCAPE AND SEASCAPE

*Earth colours and a vibrant green form the basic palette for
this watercolour of a twisting barbour wall. The tones of the
background were harmonized and blended by laying more
paint into damp washes.*

Watercolour has always been closely associated with landscape and seascape painting, and even with today's proliferation of new media for the artist there is still none more able to render the transient and atmospheric qualities of countryside, sea and sky.

◆ THE ENGLISH WATERCOLOUR ◆ TRADITION

In England, the country which more than any other can claim to have founded the great tradition of landscape painting in watercolour, landscape was not really considered a suitable subject in its own right until the late 18th century. The formal, classical landscapes of the French artists, Claude Lorraine (1600-82) and Nicolas Poussin (1594-1665), were much admired by artists and discerning collectors, as were the realistic landscapes of artists of the Dutch school such as Jacob van Ruisdael (1629-82), but the general public in the main wanted portraits and historical subjects. The great English portrait painter, Thomas Gainsborough (1727-88), had a deep love of his native landscape and regarded it as his true subject, but in order to earn a living he painted many more portraits than landscapes.

The two artists who elevated landscape and seascape to the status of fine art were Constable and Turner. Their influence on painting, not only in Great Britain but all over the world, was immeasurable. By the early 19th century landscape had arrived, and at the same time watercolour, a medium hitherto used for quick sketches and for colouring maps and prints, had become the chief medium for many landscape artists. Constable used it as his predeces-

ABOVE *Peter de Wint, an English painter of Dutch
extraction, was drawn to flat, panoramic landscapes.
His great sweeping views seem to extend beyond the
confines of the paintings themselves. Observe the sure
and confident handling of the trees and water in* Walton-
on-Thames, *and the tiny areas of unpainted paper which,
give extra sparkle to the picture.*

LEFT *Thomas Girtin was a pioneer of watercolour
painting much admired by his contemporary, Turner.
He worked with only five colours – black, monastral
blue, yellow ochre, burnt sienna and light red – to
create subtle evocations of atmosphere.* The White House,
Chelsea *shows both his fine sense of composition and his
mastery of tone and colour. In the darker areas, washes
have been laid one over another with great skill. The
focal point, the house, is slightly off-centre and has been
left as white paper, showing through with such brilliance
that it appears almost as if floodlit.*

sors had, as a rapid means of recording impressions, but Turner used it in a new and daring way and exploited its potential fully to express his feelings about light and colour.

At much the same time John Sell Cotman, the co-founder of the school of painting known as the Norwich School after its other founder, John Crome (1768-1821), who lived in that town, was producing some of the finest watercolour landscapes ever seen before or since. These paintings by the artists of the English watercolour school have never been surpassed; they became an inspiration to artists everywhere, and remain so today.

◆ PRACTICAL HINTS FOR ◆ OUTDOOR PAINTING

Once landscape had become an 'official' subject for painters, working out of doors directly from nature became increasingly common, the more so after the French Impressionists set the example. It is not now so popular. Photographers queueing up to record a beauty spot are a more usual sight than artists doing so. It is, however, an excellent discipline, which forces you to look hard at a subject and make rapid decisions about how to

treat it and lends immediacy and spontaneity to the work itself.

Watercolour is a light and portable medium, ideally suited to outdoor work, but on-the-spot painting, whatever the medium, always presents problems. Chief among them is the weather. You may have to contend with blazing heat which dries the paint as soon as it is laid down, freezing winds which numb your hands, sudden showers which blotch your best efforts or wash them away altogether, and changing light which confuses you and makes you doubt your initial drawing and composition. If the weather looks unpredictable, take extra clothes (a pair of old gloves with the fingers cut off the painting hand are a help in winter), a plastic bag or carrier large enough to hold your board in case of rain, and anything else you can think of for your comfort, such as a thermos of tea or coffee and a radio. If the sun is bright try to sit in a shaded place; otherwise the light will bounce back at you off the white paper, which makes it difficult or sometimes impossible to see what you are doing. If you are embarrassed by the comments of passers-by, a 'walkman' serves as an efficient insulation device. Some people also find it an aid to concentration, though others do not. Always take sufficient water and receptacles to put it in, and restrict your palette to as few colours as possible.

Choose a subject that genuinely interests you rather than one you feel you 'ought' to paint, even if it is only a back garden or local park. If you are familiar with a particular area you will probably already have a subject, or several subjects, in mind. On holiday in an unfamiliar place, try to assess a subject in advance by carrying out a preliminary reconaissance rather than dashing straight out with your paints. Finally, try to work as quickly as you can without rushing, so that the first important stages of the painting are complete before the light changes. If necessary make a start on one day and complete the work on another. Seascapes are especially difficult, since the colour of the sea can change drastically — from dark indigo to bright blue-green, for example — in a matter of minutes. It is often advisable to make several quick colour sketches and then work indoors from them.

ABOVE Francis Towne's work was not appreciated in the 19th century, but he has since been recognized as one of the great names of British watercolour painting. He felt a particular fascination for grand mountain landscapes, finding much of his inspiration in the wild scenery of the Alps, North Wales and England's Lake District. This painting, Grasmere by the Road, *is typical of his technique, in which pen outline is used to isolate areas of contrasting colour.*

ABOVE RIGHT A watercolour of stones at Avebury. The cool tones express the clarity of daylight and the calm grandeur of this ancient monument.

Although Turner's watercolours are less well known than his oils, they rank among his finest works. He was clearly extremely taken with watercolour and used it brilliantly and experimentally to express his preoccupation with light and atmosphere, often making use of the semi-accidental effects that occur in watercolour painting. In Venice from the Giudecca he has created distance by using thin layers of paint and cool blues in the background; the darker and warmer details in the foreground are suggested lightly enough to retain the feeling of hazy, shimmering light.

♦ SUMMER PAINTING ♦

This landscape is a fine evocation of the drama of the ever-changing countryside, here seen under the kind of summer squall of rain which causes the sky and hills to merge into one another. Watercolour is an ideal medium for capturing such atmospheric effects, but although the painting looks spontaneous (as the artist intended) it is actually very carefully planned.

The technique could not be more dissimilar to that used in the following example. Here an unusually large selection of colours has been used, and they have been deliberately allowed to mix on the paper to create soft, blurring effects. The natural translucence of watercolour has been exploited to the full to allow the bright colours, such as the greens of the foreground and the patch of sunlight on the hills, to shine out with brilliance and clarity.

Since the time of Turner the effects of light have been among the prime concerns of landscape painters, particularly those living in the temperate zones, where the landscape is subject to sudden changes. It is not easy, however, to capture light and atmosphere with brushes and paints, and a painting like this one relies for its success on a deliberate use of certain techniques as well as on fast working — freshness and spontaneity is quickly destroyed if the brushwork becomes too laboured. Here the brush strokes themselves form an integral part of the painting, having been used to suggest the uneven shroud of rain, with brighter and darker colours laid on in places with great accuracy and assurance. There are no totally flat washes anywhere in the painting. Even in the distant hills different tones and colours are visible, but a feeling of space and recession has been rendered by the use of very bright colours and greater tonal contrasts in the foreground.

MATERIALS USED

- ♦ SUPPORT: pre-stretched watercolour paper with a Not surface, measuring 9½ × 13 in/24 × 33 cm.
- ♦ COLOURS: Hooker's green, oxide of chromium, Indian yellow, Naples yellow, raw sienna, raw umber, cobalt blue, ultramarine and permanent rose, plus a little Chinese white.
- ♦ BRUSHES: a selection of soft brushes and a small household brush.

1

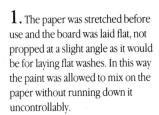

1. The paper was stretched before use and the board was laid flat, not propped at a slight angle as it would be for laying flat washes. In this way the paint was allowed to mix on the paper without running down it uncontrollably.

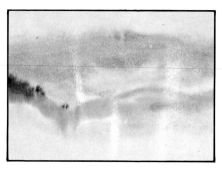

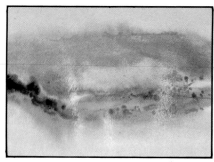

2. As the first colours began to dry slightly a warmer pink tone was introduced to the sky and touches of blue added to the middle distance. In this technique, called working wet into wet, the paint is never allowed to dry entirely; but if new paint is added when the first layer is too wet it will flood rather than merge softly into the other colours.

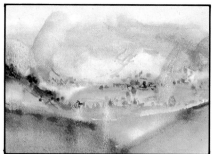

3. A broad bristle-brush was used to block in the colours for the foreground, the greens being chosen to balance the yellow-green patch of sunlight on the hills. Oil-painting brushes and household brushes can often be used in watercolour painting to create particular effects.

4. Next, bold brush strokes were introduced into the sky to indicate the rain clouds, and the sky was given a yellow hue and then overlaid with grey-blue. At the same time the foreground colours were strengthened and further definition was added.

5. Finished painting: to give a softer, more blurred, effect to the rain a little white was added to the paint in the final stages. Adding white to watercolour gives an effect quite unlike the harsher one provided by gouache paints, but it should not be used until the painting is near completion; otherwise it may muddy the other colours.

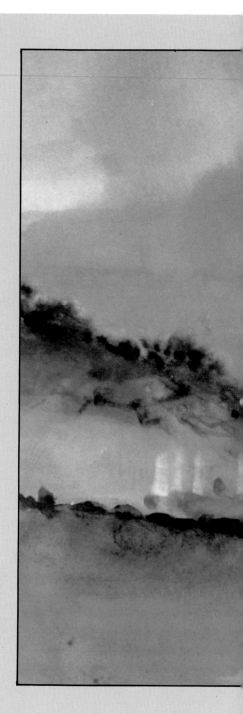

Raw Umber   *Cobalt Blue*

Summer Painting

Ultramarine   *Permanent Rose*   *Hooker's Green*   *Oxide of Chromium*   *Indian Yellow*   *Naples Yellow*   *Raw Sienna*

1

◆ DISTANT HILLS ◆

This painting relies for its effect on the use of linear shapes arranged in such a way as to create an atmosphere of gentle harmony. The colour range is very limited, almost monochromatic, and the minimum of detail, even in the foreground, gives the elegantly uncluttered and stylized look characteristic of many Chinese paintings.

One of the artist's main concerns was to indicate the spaciousness and recession of the landscape. He used two methods to do this. The first was aerial perspective, the term used for the way that the features of a landscape become less distinct as they recede, with the colours becoming paler and cooler. Tonal contrasts are greater in the foreground, where the colours are strong and warm. The second method was to allow the tree on the right to go out of the frame at the top, thus clearly indicating that the group of trees is on the picture plane (the front of the painting).

The painting provides an excellent example of the 'classical' approach to watercolour, in which the paint is laid on in a series of thin washes, allowing the brilliance of the white paper to reflect back through them. Unusually, an HP (hot-pressed) paper was used instead of the more popular Not, or cold-pressed, but this artist finds that the smoother paper suits his style, and he mixes a little gum arabic with the water to give extra body and adherence. Each wash, once laid down, has been left without any further paint being laid on top, and the painting was worked from the top downward, with the foreground trees painted over the washes for the sky and hills. It was done in the studio from a sketch and the drawing on the support was restricted to a few lines drawn with an HB pencil.

1. This photograph gives an idea of how much paint is needed for a wash over a large area. Until you are used to laying washes it is wise to mix more than you think you will need. This wash, for the sky, is diluted cobalt blue.

2. The wash for the sky, put on with a No.10 squirrel brush, was deliberately laid slightly unevenly to suggest a pale blue sky with a light cloud cover.

3. As soon as the wash for the sky was dry, the same squirrel brush was used to put on a darker shade, with Payne's grey added to the cobalt blue, to the area of the far hills.

4. The second wash had to be darker than that for the sky but not too dark, as the artist knew that he would have to increase the tonal contrasts in the middle distance to suggest its relative nearness to the picture plane.

5 and 6. As each wash has to be allowed to dry before putting on the next, in this particular technique, a hairdrier is sometimes used to hasten the process. The third and fourth washes, darker shades of the second, were laid on next, leaving the whole of the foreground and middle distance still untouched.

7. The tone of the darker area of the middle distance had to be very carefully calculated to make it appear to be in front of the far hills. This wash has been put on slightly thicker in places to suggest the shapes of the trees.

8. The trees in the foreground were worked on next, the darker paint being taken over the background and sky washes. This overlapping device is most successful when the colours are similar; overlapping two quite different colours, for instance red-brown tree trunks over a bright green middle distance, would give a third colour, which could provide a jarring element if not planned.

9 and 10. At this stage both the background and foreground were complete, but the area between the two was still unpainted. Because warm colours tend to advance and cool ones recede, the artist laid a warm greenish wash over this area to make it come forward toward the picture plane.

MATERIALS USED

♦ SUPPORT: pre-stretched watercolour paper with an HP surface, measuring 14 × 21½ in/35 × 53 cm.
♦ COLOURS: cobalt blue, Payne's grey, raw umber and sap green.
♦ BRUSHES: a No. 10 squirrel and a No. 4 sable.
♦ ADDITIONAL EQUIPMENT: a selection of ceramic palettes for mixing the paint; a little gum arabic for mixing with the water.

Distant Hills

1. Having made a careful outline drawing of the main shapes, the artist blocked out the brightest areas of the rocks with masking fluid. This method highlights the importance of an accurate drawing, since the artist has to know from the outset exactly where to place the masking fluid.

♦ OLD HARRY AND HIS WIFE ♦

A large variety of different techniques has been used to create the deceptively simple effect of this painting. The subject is bold and dramatic, and its drama has been emphasized by the juxtaposition of large, solid shapes. The tonal contrasts between the rocks and the sea are distinct enough for the rocks to stand out as light against dark, but not so great as to spoil the delicate balance. Greater contrasts might have looked overstated.

Seascapes can be tricky subjects. It is difficult to decide whether to treat the sea as a flat area or to try to show the movement of the water by 'filling in' every wave and ripple. Also, when painting outdoors, you will see the colours constantly changing, which can give rise to uncertainty about the best approach. Here the sea has been treated fairly flat, with just enough unevenness and broken texture to suggest water; the sky hints at clouds, nothing more. The artist did not have to contend with changing colours and lights, since the painting was done in the studio. He used a photograph as his main reference for the shapes and was thus free to decide on a colour scheme without external distraction. The light falling on the rock, which the photograph features very vividly, has been given a minor role in the painting, as the artist was more concerned with the texture of the rock, which is echoed in the rippling reflection below.

Masking fluid provided the ideal way of dealing with the rock. The brightly lit areas were covered with the fluid, so that the shadow areas could be built up without the paints encroaching on the highlights. In places the dry-brush technique was used, together with that of spattering the paint. Both techniques are excellent for suggesting texture, though they should always be used sparingly.

2. Masking fluid gives a different effect from that obtained by painting around areas to be reserved. The marks of the brush are visible when the fluid is removed, thus making it a method of painting in 'negative'. When the masking fluid was dry, a broken wash was laid over the sky area and then a darker one for the line of distant cliffs.

3. The sea was laid in with a soft brush and a dilute wash of Payne's grey. This wash was deliberately kept loose and fluid, and the paint was moved around to create different tones.

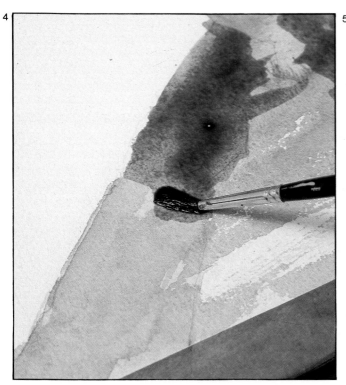

4. Here the artist is using a darker tone of Payne's grey, mixed with ultramarine, a warm blue, to darken the sea in places.

5. At this stage the entire surface has been covered and the masking fluid, yellowish in colour, is still on. A pale wash of lemon yellow was laid on the reflection area and greyish washes put over the darker parts of the rocks.

6. Using diluted black paint, the artist works the darkest shadows between the rocks and at the bottom of the central rock.

7. Once the dark tones have been put on, the masking fluid is removed by rubbing gently with the finger. Masking fluid is not suitable for use on rough paper, as it sinks into the hollows and cannot be removed.

8. The grassy tops of the cliffs are now painted sap green with a fine brush. Note how the artist darkens the colour at the edge to produce a crisp line of shadow.

9. Here the artist is preparing the brush for dry-brush work by spreading the bristles below the ferrule so that they will give a series of fine lines. The minimum of paint is put on the brush for this technique.

10. Another technique used for this painting was to cover an area already painted with gummed water, leave it to dry, and then gently work into it with a brush dipped in clear water to give small areas of lighter tone.

11. Here the artist is using a broad bristle-brush to spatter paint on to the surface. Surrounding areas were masked off first. This is an effective texture-creating technique, but care must be taken to mix a colour which is only slightly darker than that underneath; otherwise you will create a spotted, rather than an unobtrusively textured, effect.

12. As a final touch, the line of wavelets at the bottom of the rocks is added with opaque white paint, which is allowed to mix a little with the blue to give the broken effect of foamy water.

MATERIALS USED

♦ SUPPORT: pre-stretched watercolour paper with a Not surface, measuring 21 × 30 in/54 × 75 cm.

♦ COLOURS: black, Payne's grey, ultramarine, cobalt blue, sap green, lemon yellow, yellow ochre and raw umber, plus a little white gouache.

♦ BRUSHES AND OTHER EQUIPMENT: a selection of large and small soft brushes, a broad bristle-brush, gum arabic, masking fluid and masking tape.

Old Harry and His Wife

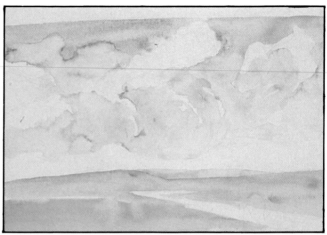

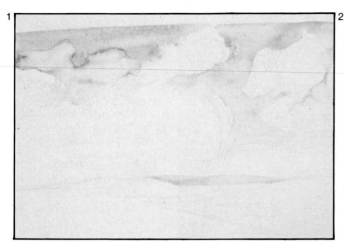

1. The artist started with some pencil lines to indicate the position of the horizon and the diagonal line of the river. He then began to lay wet washes on the sky and distant hills, using the brush as a drawing implement to describe the shapes of the clouds.

2. The artist continued to build up wet washes, keeping the middle ground fairly light at this stage, and repeating the warm pink tones on the undersides of the clouds.

3. The hills on the left have now been deepened in tone, so that they separate themselves from the more distant hills behind. At the same time further modelling has been added to the clouds by building up the mid-tones with Payne's grey, warm blue-grey and pink.

♦ CLOUDS ♦

In a landscape painting, sky and land should always be seen together and in relation to one another, since the particular light cast by the sky — varying according to the amount of cloud cover and the position of the sun — has a direct influence on the colours and tones of the land below. Also, the shapes and colours of clouds can be used as an important part of a composition, perhaps to act as a counterfoil to some feature of the foreground or to echo a shape or colour in the middle distance.

Watercolour lends itself very well to sky painting, since by working wet into wet effects can often be produced which resemble those seen in skies. Care must be taken, however, not to allow too many hard edges to form or the soft, rounded appearance of the clouds will be lost. Here the artist has kept the paint quite loose and fluid, using the brush to draw the cloud shapes and laying one wash over another to build up the forms. He has worked all over the painting at the same time, repeating some of the warm pinky-browns of the foreground and middle distance in the clouds themselves, so that the painting has a feeling of unity, with no artificial division between sky and land. The horizon has been placed quite low, as the sky is the main focus of interest.

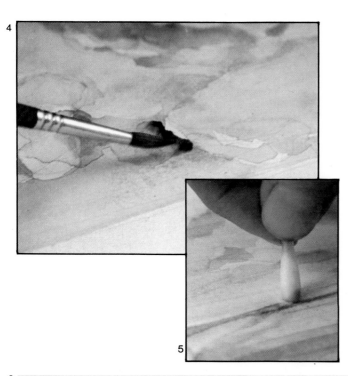

4. Here the artist is seen working wet into wet, adding small touches of Payne's grey to parts of the clouds. Notice how the fine lines which have formed in places where the paint has flooded have been cleverly exploited to give a crisp look to the clouds.

5. Sponges and cotton buds are particularly useful for a painting like this, as they can be used to soften edges, as here, or to draw paler shapes into an existing wash.

6. The final touches, which have brought the whole painting together, were to add some definition to the foreground and to increase the intensity of the blue above the clouds, so that the darker tones of land and sky are pleasingly balanced.

MATERIALS USED

♦ SUPPORT: pre-stretched watercolour paper, measuring 10 × 14 in/25 × 35 cm.
♦ COLOURS: ultramarine, cobalt blue, olive green, burnt sienna, cadmium yellow, alizarin crimson, Payne's grey.
♦ BRUSHES AND OTHER EQUIPMENT: Nos. 12, 8 and 4 soft brushes, cotton buds.

Clouds

CHAPTER SIX

BUILDINGS

Bonington's paintings, in both oil and watercolour, were much admired in his lifetime. He died of consumption at the age of 26 without having fully exploited his gift. As a colourist he was superb, and he was a pioneer in the use of watercolour, but it is said of him that he never fully understood perspective. In this painting, Castelbarco Tomb, the subject is sufficiently simple to disguise any possible weakness, and it comes across as a bold and dramatic statement of form and colour.

ALTHOUGH PAINTINGS which take a building or a group of buildings as their subject are usually regarded as a branch of landscape painting, it is more practical to regard architectural painting and drawing as a separate subject. It presents its own problems, not the least of them being the intricacies of perspective. Obviously not all paintings of buildings need be as accurate and precise as an architect's drawings — this is seldom desirable — but a painting of a house, church or ruin is similar to a portrait. It is that particular building you want to paint, because you are attracted to its shape, colour or general atmosphere. It is therefore important to get the proportions and perspective right, just as you would the features of a face.

♦ THE TOPOGRAPHICAL TRADITION ♦

Before the time of the great watercolour landscape painters of the later 18th and early 19th centuries, watercolour had been used mainly for quick sketches and topographical drawings, that is, precise visual records of landscapes or buildings. Many such drawings and paintings were intended as the basis for engravings or etchings, and were not really painterly in approach, colour being used in flat washes to supplement a linear drawing, often in pen and ink. In the 19th century interest in buildings was stimulated by the comparative ease of travel to foreign parts. Crumbling medieval ruins, Roman remains and picturesque streets in old towns became favourite subjects for artists. By then, too, the use of watercolour had become much more daring and inventive, and artists were concerned with conveying the feeling and atmosphere of buildings, not simply recording their outward appearance and superficial details as an architect or draughtsman

would. Paintings such as Bonington's *Castelbarco Tomb* and Turner's *Tintern Abbey* are faithful and accurate records of the buildings, but they are also full of life and vigour, thus combining the topographical tradition with that of poetic landscape.

♦ PRACTICAL HINTS ♦

Some knowledge of perspective is needed to make a building look solid and convincing, but the most important factor is close and careful observation, which leads to a good foundation drawing. Try to work directly from the subject itself wherever possible: photographs, which distort the perspective, are not the ideal source of reference for architectural subjects. A photograph taken with a standard instant camera, which usually has a wide-angle lens (35–45mm focal length) will cause a tall building to look much shorter and wider; and any details in shadow, such as the top of a wall under the eaves of a roof, will probably be indistinguishable.

Watercolourists of the past sometimes paid a draughtsman to make a preliminary drawing for them. They would simply put on the colour! Most of us, however, have to do our own donkey-work, and with a complicated subject it can take time. Fortunately, the drawing can be done on one day (and can take as long as necessary, since changing light does not matter very much at this stage) and the actual painting on another, or even indoors. A photograph might then be used as a reference for the colour only.

A small ruler is a useful addition to your usual drawing kit as it can be used to check angles, verticals and horizontals by holding it up at arm's length and to draw guidelines on the paper. There is no reason why all drawing should be done freehand; the rather mechanical-looking lines

LEFT Turner was a master of every kind of painting he turned his hand to, and he could portray the intricate details of a building with the same skill and sensitivity that he brought to atmospheric landscapes. This detail from his Study of Tintern Abbey *shows a combination of the topographical draughtman's precision and the painter's eye for mood, tone and colour.*

Seaside Pavilion, *by Moira Clinch, is a good example of an intricately detailed architectural study which nevertheless retains the freshness and sparkle of more spontaneous sketches. Light and shade are cleverly handled, the clear, fresh, pale colours of the regular squares of paving stones providing a pleasing contrast to the deeper blues of the sky and parts of the building. On the pavilion itself every minute detail of the position itself has been recorded with faithful accuracy, yet the painting nowhere looks overworked or tired.*

given by ruling will be obscured once the paint is laid on. Proportions can be measured by the pencil-and-thumb method, and all such measurements should be constantly checked and re-assessed as the work progresses.

Once the painting itself is begun, you can work in a much freer manner, altering small details to improve the composition. But architecture generally calls for a more methodical approach than landscape. Lines usually need to be crisp and clear. So allow each wash to dry before putting on the next, turning the board sideways or upside down, if need be, to fill in each area.

When the first washes have been laid on, texture, such as that of brickwork or stone, can be suggested by any of the various methods described in Chapter 3 and small, precise details can be added carefully with a fine brush. Final touches are often added with a pencil or pen and ink to give a crisp definition to the painting, but they must be handled carefully. A heavy, black line can destroy the delicacy of a painting.

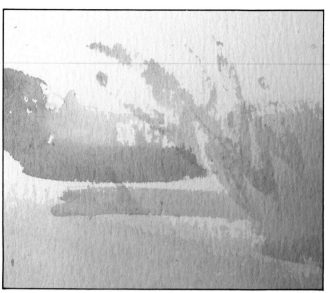

6. Here the artist is defining the shadows on the unlit sides of the buildings, allowing the paint to mix on the paper in order to produce a soft effect.

7. He uses a combination of Prussian blue and Payne's grey to achieve relatively strong tonal contrasts.

8. The paint was kept quite fluid throughout the painting, and the texture of the paper is an important element in the final effect. Here a large, soft brush is used to apply dark green over the light red of the roofs and the blue of the sky, so that the colours blend into one another in a pleasing way.

9. The lines of the vines are laid on with bold brush strokes and darkened in places to hint at shadow, without describing it in detail. Strong tonal contrasts help to bring the foreground forward toward the picture plane.

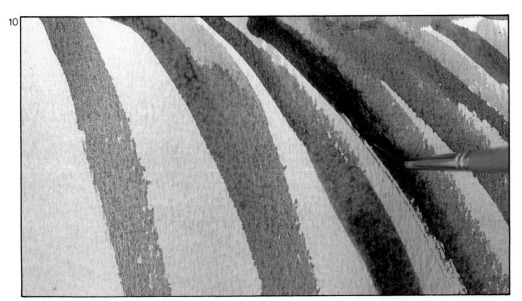

10

10. The rows of vines are reinforced with a mixture of terre verte and Payne's grey. Shadows are not usually merely darker shades of the same colour, but have their own colours.

MATERIALS USED

- SUPPORT: pre-stretched watercolour paper with a Not surface, measuring 12 × 16 in/30 × 40 cm.
- COLOURS: raw umber, burnt umber, Payne's grey, terre verte, Hooker's green, yellow ochre, permanent yellow, Prussian blue and cadmium red.
- BRUSHES: Nos. 4 and 11 sable.

Vineyard in Italy

♦ CHURCH IN FRANCE ♦

Buildings present special problems to the artist, especially the watercolourist, and they demand a fairly precise and planned method of approach. In a painting such as this, where the church is the *raison d'être* of the picture rather than being just one feature in a landscape, the perspective must be convincing, the lines sharp and clear, and some suggestion made of the texture and quality of the masonry.

This artist has worked in a very deliberate way, starting with a careful outline drawing made with a sharp pencil and ruler to map out the main areas, so that he is sure where to place his first wash. He then put on a series of flat washes, the first one being laid over the sky area and the second, very pale, over the building itself. Next he began to consider the best way of suggesting the stonework, and decided on masking fluid, applied in slightly uneven brush

strokes. When this was dry he washed over the top with brownish grey paint and then removed the fluid, leaving lines of paint between and around the original brush strokes. Further texture was applied at a later stage by the spattering method, and crisp lines were given to details, such as the face and hands of the clock, by drawing with a sharp pencil. The whole painting has a pleasing crispness, produced by the very sharply defined areas of light and dark; no attempt has been made to blend the paint in the shadow areas, and very distinct tonal contrasts have been used — in the small round tree in front of the church, for example. The artist has also avoided the temptation to put in too much detail, which might have reduced the impact and made the picture look fussy and untidy. The tiled roof consists simply of a flat wash; although there is just enough variation in the sky to avoid a mechanical look, no attempt has been made to paint actual clouds.

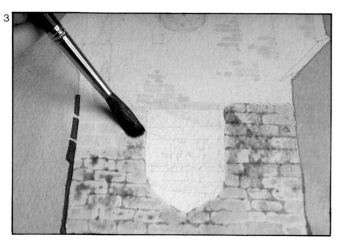

1 and 2. In a subject like this a careful outline drawing is essential. Once the drawing was complete the artist laid an almost flat wash over the sky and then a paler one over the building. These established his basic mid-tones, enabling him to gauge the tonal strength of the steeple.

3. The steeple was painted and allowed to dry, after which masking fluid was put on to areas of the masonry, not as a flat wash but as individual brush strokes. Fairly dark brownish paint was washed over this when dry so that it sank into the areas between the brush strokes.

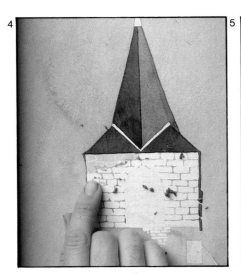

4. Here the masking fluid is being rubbed off with a finger, leaving the irregular lines of dark paint to suggest the edges of the stones. This is a more effective method than painting in the lines, and gives a much more natural look because the technique is a very slightly 'random' one.

5. Here the spattering technique is being used to give further texture to the walls. It is sometimes necessary to mask off surrounding areas so that they do not get splashed, but this artist makes use of the method quite often, and is confident of his ability to control the paint.

6. At this stage only the foreground, with the dark trees and bright grass, remain unpainted. The artist worked the painting piece by piece, as he found that having no overlapping layers of paint gave a crisper definition, but it is not a method recommended for beginners because it is difficult to judge tones and colours in isolation.

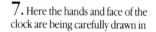

7. Here the hands and face of the clock are being carefully drawn in with a very sharp pencil over the original pale wash.

8. Further texture is given to the stonework by rubbing a candle over the paint. Candles or wax crayon can also be used as a resist method, like masking fluid, in which case they are applied before a final paint layer.

9. The mid-tones of the grass have now been laid in, providing a foil to the red-brown of the tiled roof.

10. The artist now works carefully on the shadow side of the tree, using a fine brush and very dense dark green paint.

11. The final touches were to darken the left hand tree and paint in the straight, dark shadow in the foreground. Two small trees were also added in the shadow area at the bottom of the church.

MATERIALS USED

- ♦ SUPPORT: pre-stretched 200 lb Bockingford paper
- ♦ BRUSHES: Nos. 2, 7 and 9 sables and a 1-in/2.5 cm bristle brush for spattering.
- ♦ COLOURS: cobalt blue, sap green, yellow ochre, raw umber, brown madder alizarin, Payne's grey and ivory black
- ♦ ADDITIONAL EQUIPMENT: masking fluid, a candle and gum water.

11

Church in France

CHAPTER SEVEN

NATURE

Dürer's accurate and precise drawings and watercolours of plants and animals are possibly the best examples of natural-history painting in the entire history of art. The Young Hare was probably begun with broad washes of transparent paint to establish the main form. The fine details were then built up with tiny brush strokes of opaque paint; every hair and whisker has been precisely described, but the hare is still quite evidently a living, breathing creature.

*F*ROM THE 16TH CENTURY onwards watercolour became a favoured medium for botanical illustration, which, with the great upsurge of interest in describing and cataloguing plants and flowers, was very much in demand. Just as it did for architecture, the medium proved ideal for the detailed and delicate work demanded by such subjects.

♦ NATURAL-HISTORY PAINTING ♦

In the early years of the 16th century Dürer pioneered the use of watercolour with body colour for botanical subjects, and such works as *The Great Piece of Turf* and *Young Hare*, faithful renderings of nature, laid the basis for a tradition of botanical and natural-history painting which has continued down to the present day.

In the 18th and 19th centuries the majority of natural-history painters and illustrators made their initial watercolours as bases for engravings. Some, notably the famous French flower painter, Pierre-Joseph Redouté (1759-1840), mastered the art of engraving themselves, the techniques of which in turn influenced styles of painting. In America natural-history painting in watercolour reached new heights with the marvellous bird paintings of John James Audubon (1785-1851), paintings which became familiar to a wide public through the hand-coloured engravings done from them. These works, although they are in the illustrative tradition of accurate observation, are now regarded as art rather than illustration (there is really no dividing line between the two) and change hands at staggering prices.

Watercolour is still much used for precise botanical and natural-history illustration, but it has also come into its own as a medium for depicting nature, particularly flowers, in a more painterly way, either in its natural environment or in the studio as still-life.

The painting of water-lilies overleaf shows how superbly the medium can be used to give a feeling of life and immediacy: the water-lilies could almost be opening before your eyes.

♦ PRACTICAL HINTS ♦

Flowers and plants always make attractive subjects and present no particular problems other than the usual one of getting the drawing right. However, many people frequently buy a bunch of flowers and paint them at home, but do not think of going out to paint them in their natural environment. There is nothing at all wrong with the still-life approach. Countless superb paintings have been done of plants and flowers indoors. But painting or drawing on the spot is an excellent way of observing nature, and the plants or flowers do tend to look more at home in their natural setting.

Ring-tailed Lemur, *by Sally Michel, has something of the quality of Dürer's work. She works in watercolour and* pastel, and always from life, though she takes the occasional polaroid for reference.

Sally Michel

This study of waterlilies, by Marc Winer, was painted on the spot, with much use of the wet-into-wet technique. The artist allowed some colours to run into one another in a semi-random way, sometimes creating hard edges, sometimes more gentle transitions, an effective way to suggest the soft wetness of the leaves and flowers floating in water.

Animals and birds present much graver problems to the would-be wild-life painter. They simply will not sit still. For most professional wild-life artists, birds or animals are a life-long passion, and they have often made a long study of their chosen subject from books and museums before beginning to sketch and observe from nature. A family pet, however, can often be prevailed upon to stay in one place for long enough to be sketched — especially if it has just had a good meal — and photographs can sometimes be used in combination with sketches as the basis for a painting. Anyone who decides to make animals or birds his subject should try to observe them as often and as closely as possible, both in movement and in repose. You may think you know exactly what your dog or cat looks like, but if you try to daw it from memory you will soon realize the limits of your knowledge.

◆ TROPICAL FISH ◆

It can be difficult to find natural-history subjects that remain still for long enough to be observed and studied by the artist, but fish in a tank almost beg to be looked at and admired, and although they are always on the move, at least they do not move very far. Many wild-life artists make a particular branch of the animal world their own, often because of a life-long interest. This artist has studied fish very closely, and has made a great many drawings of them over the years.

The painting was done from a series of drawings and from past observations of the structure and colours of the fish. It makes use of both the wet-into-wet technique, in which new colour is applied to a wash before it is dry, and the wet-into-dry technique, in which wet washes are laid over dry ones so that they overlap in places. The hard and soft edges formed in this way create the illusion of rippling water, a very important element in the painting. The background washes had to be applied extremely carefully and accurately so that they did not spoil the crisp edges of the fishes' bodies and fins. A careful drawing was made before any paint was put on.

Although people often think of watercolours as pale and delicate, the colours can be made as vivid as you like, simply by being less diluted. In places the artist has used the paint almost pure to create bright and glowing effects. She has also used complementary colours to good effect: the bright oranges of the fish are accentuated by the complementary greenish-browns in the background.

1. This sketch is just one of many that the artist has made in the past and uses as reference for her paintings.

2. Having made a careful drawing on her stretched paper with a sharp pencil, the artist began by painting in the shapes of the fish with a mixture of cadmium orange and cadmium yellow pale. The colours and tones were varied to show the lights and darks of the bodies as well as the individual differences between the fish. Some of the broader details were drawn into the bodies before the first wash was dry, giving a soft effect.

3. The background colour was a mixture of black and lemon yellow, which gives a warmer colour than blue and yellow. When laying the wash the artist took special care to work precisely and accurately between and around the fins and bodies in order to preserve the clean, crisp lines that are such a vital feature of the painting.

4. When the broad area of the background has been laid in with deliberately uneven washes to suggest ripples, the painting was allowed to dry. Further layers of colour were then added, so that the water became darker around the fish and lighter at the top, where the proportion of yellow to black was increased.

5. Here the artist is painting the leaves with a fine brush in a very strong lemon yellow, barely diluted. This covers the original pale wash and is slightly modified by it.

6. A very fine sable brush was used to paint the delicate details of the scales, and touches of white were added in places. When doing detailed work in the centre of a painting, make sure the area below is quite dry or you may ruin the painting by smudging it.

◆ PHEASANT ◆

This painting is both a bird study and still-life, since it was painted indoors and the subject is a stuffed pheasant borrowed from an antique shop. Artists whose particular interest is wildlife can study and observe nature at second hand as well as directly from life. Natural-history books and museums both offer opportunities for gaining a thorough knowledge about structure and detail.

Because there could be no attempt to make the stuffed bird appear anything other than what it was, the painting presented a different challenge from that of representing a live bird. With a live bird the prime consideration might have been to suggest movement, while the natural background of trees or rocks might have formed part of the composition. Here the artist chose to treat the subject in a very formal way, setting it up as a rather stark still-life, but his enthusiasm for the bird itself comes across very strongly in the glowing colour and the delicately painted detail.

His technique was quite free and fluid, and he worked quickly, building up the form in the early stages from loose washes and working wet into wet in places. The background shows an interesting use of watercolour: with only one colour a wide variety of tonal contrasts has been achieved. This gives the painting extra drama and excitement as well as providing a balance to the texture of the pheasant itself.

1. A very hard (F) pencil was used to make a careful outline drawing to establish the forms of the bird as well as its relationship to the background and table-top. Composition is extremely important for this subject, which relies for its impact on the way the main shape is placed. Once he had planned the composition, allowing the tail to go out of the frame so that it appears longer, the artist first laid a pale wash on the body and tail.

2. Once the first wash, a mixture of raw umber and cadmium orange, was dry, a darker one using using the same colours was laid on top, after which blue and red were applied to the head and neck.

3. The same red, alizarin crimson, was put on the breast area, and the artist then began to work on the head feathers with a fine brush. He used a mixture of black, viridian and ultramarine for this, leaving parts of the original blue showing through.

4. Some artists work all over a painting at the same time, but in this painting the bird was completed before the artist turned his attention to the background. Here the feathers are being painted, with the paint kept quite loose and fluid to prevent a cramped, overworked look.

5. This detail shows the richness and variety of both the colours and the brushwork. In the red area a darker tone has been allowed to overlap the one below, creating a series of edges which give the impression of feathers. Note how small lines of white have been left in the original wash to stand for the wing feathers.

6. The painting of the bird is now complete, and the successive washes built up one over the other have created exactly the rich impression that the artist wanted. When putting washes over other washes in this way it is essential to know when to stop; if the surface of the paper becomes too clogged with paint the painting will begin to look tired. Judging the strength of colour needed for each wash takes some practice, since watercolour looks so much darker when it is wet.

7. Now the artist begins to work on the background, using a fairly strong mixture of Payne's grey and taking it very carefully around the bird's body. It is often necessary to turn the board sideways or upside down for this kind of work.

MATERIALS USED

♦ SUPPORT: pre-stretched Bockingford watercolour paper, measuring 22 × 30 in/55 × 75 cm.
♦ COLOURS: chrome orange, alizarin crimson, burn sienna, raw umber, ultramarine, viridian, Payne's grey and black.
♦ BRUSHES: Nos. 12 and 2 sable and a No. 7 synthetic round.

8. By varying the tones of the background wash the artist has made the bird stand out in a very three-dimensional way. The dark head is prevented from merging into the similar tone behind it by the thin line of white which has been left between the two. The white area of the table-top has been carefully placed so that it is not quite central and thus provides a balance to the long, almost horizontal, line of the tail.

Pheasant

◆ GERANIUM ◆

This painting demonstrates very well how in the right hands watercolour can be an ideal medium for capturing the rich colours and strong, yet intricate, forms of flowers and foliage. The starting-point was a single bloom in a garden trough, but the artist has transformed the rather ordinary subject seen in the photograph into a highly dramatic painting with a strong element of abstract pattern. He has reduced the background to an area of dark neutral colour, which allows the shapes of the leaves to stand out in bold contrast, but he has given it interest by varying the tonal contrasts while using only one colour. He has done this by allowing the paint and water to mix unevenly, and even form blobs in places, and by scrubbing the paint with a stiff household brush.

Although no preliminary drawing was done, the artist had a very clear idea of the composition before he began to paint; the positioning of the flowers against the background is a vital element in the effect of the painting. The leaves have been slightly cropped by the frame on both sides, thereby bringing the flowers and leaves towards the picture plane. The almost horizontal band of lighter colour in the foreground, suggesting the garden trough, adds to this effect, firmly 'mooring' the plant in the front of the picture. It is interesting to compare the finished painting with the penultimate stage, in which the flower appears to float in space.

1. The colours were built up gradually from very light to very dark, and the first step was to apply dilute washes of green and red to the leaves and flower head.

2. The leaves were then darkened in places and touches of cerulean blue added to the flower head with a No. 2 sable brush.

3. Once the main shapes of the leaves and flower had been established, the artist began to paint the background, using a mixture of Payne's grey and cerulean blue and judging the tones very carefully. Assessing the strength of a dark wash takes practice, as watercolour appears much lighter when it is dry.

4. Next the artist began to darken the tones on some of the leaves, mixing the Payne's grey used for the background with cadmium green. Using only a small selection of colours helps to give unity to a painting.

5. Payne's grey was again used, this time pure, to paint the fine, delicate lines formed by the stems and veins of the leaves. A No. 2 sable brush gave the fine brushmarks needed for this detailed work.

EXPLOITING THE WASH.

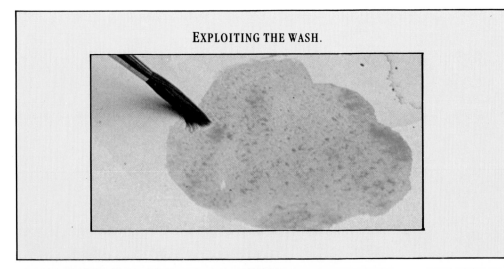

The general leaf shapes were produced with a very wet green wash. The paint was then drawn out, while still wet, into thin strands to create the leaf stems.

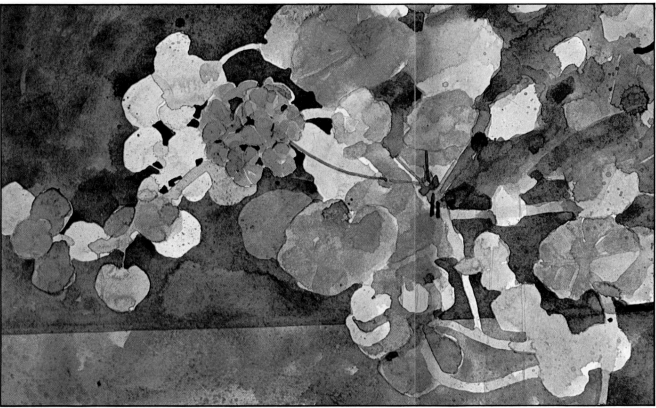

6 The red of the flower head had to be as vivid as possible, and the depth of colour was achieved by laying deep washes of vermilion over paler ones in which a little blue had been added. Note how the artist has varied the intensity of the colours and left small lines of a lighter tone showing through to suggest the shapes of the petals.

Geranium

MATERIALS USED

♦ SUPPORT: pre-stretched watercolour paper with a Not surface, measuring 18 × 23 in/45 × 57 cm.
♦ COLOURS: vermilion, yellow ochre, cadmium green, Payne's grey, cerulean blue and black.
♦ BRUSHES: Nos. 10, 6 and 2 sables and a small household brush for the background.

◆ FIELD OF DAISIES ◆

There is no better medium than watercolour for rendering the bright colours and delicate detail of flowers, but a painting like this one presents a technical problem which is not easy to overcome by traditional methods. Since watercolour must always be worked dark over light, white or pale shades are created by painting around them. Here the white shapes are smaller and more intricate than they are in most paintings, and if the artist had attempted to lay washes around them the painting would have run the risk of becoming niggly and tired-looking. He has solved this problem by using masking fluid for the heads of the flowers, laying washes of varying intensities on top and then removing the fluid to reveal the white paper.

Some artists find masking fluid a rather mechanical device, and in the past it was more often used for illustration and other graphic work, but in fact it can be used quite freely, as it was in this painting, and can either be applied with a brush or used for spattering effects. It is difficult to draw really fine lines with it, however, as it is thick and viscous. The artist has therefore used oil pastel to draw the stems of the flowers. This works as a resist medium in the same way as masking fluid; the oil repels the water, creating clear lines and interesting textures.

One of the most difficult decisions faced by painters attempting plant or flower studies outdoors is what to put in and leave out. Obviously, if you try to include every flower head and blade of grass, as well as large parts of background and sky, the painting will become a confused jumble.

A comparison of this painting with the reference photograph shows how the artist has simplified the subject, reducing the number of flowers to make a telling arrangement and allowing the background to become simply a dark, receding area suggestive of grass. No preliminary drawing was done, as the artist wanted to create a feeling of spontaneity, but less experienced painters would probably find an advance thumbnail sketch or two helpful in establishing the composition.

1. Without making a drawing on the support, the artist began by picking out the flower heads with masking fluid. Since this takes some time to dry, it should always be done in the very early stages.

2. Here the artist is using oil pastel to draw the stems, keeping the strokes as free as possible. When the watercolour washes are applied, the paint will slide off the pastel, leaving a clear line.

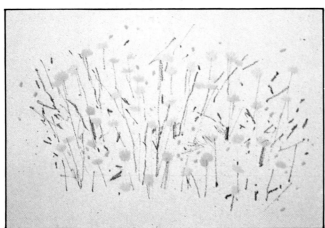

3. Before any paint was put on, the artist established the overall pattern with masking fluid and with lines and dots of oil pastel.

4. Next the whole picture area was covered with a wash of sap green and yellow, deliberately applied unevenly and loosely. The brush strokes, made with a No. 6 sable brush, were used to suggest the movement of wind-blown grass and leaves.

TEXTURING.
The green wash is enlivened by the strong brush strokes. This is purely a textural effect: note that the colour is exactly the same as the first.

5. Once the first wash was laid, the artist began to strengthen the colour in places with a dark mixture of chrome green and black. A slight sheen was given to the paint by mixing it with gum water.

6

REMOVING MASKING FLUID.

Before removing masking fluid (by gently rubbing with the finger, as the artist does here), ensure that the paint is quite dry and that no further alterations or additions are needed.

6. The deepest shadows in the foreground have now been painted and the background has been darkened. The darker green areas were carefully drawn with a fine brush, as more accurate definition was needed at this stage.

7. The final touch was to paint in the flower centres with cadmium yellow.

MATERIALS USED

♦ SUPPORT: Arches watercolour paper with a Not surface, measuring 12 × 18 in/ 30 × 45 cm.
♦ COLOURS: watercolours in sap green, chrome green, cadmium yellow and black; oil pastels in olive green and yellow.
♦ BRUSHES AND OTHER EQUIPMENT: Nos. 6 and 4 sable brushes, a small household brush for spattering, gum water and masking fluid.

7

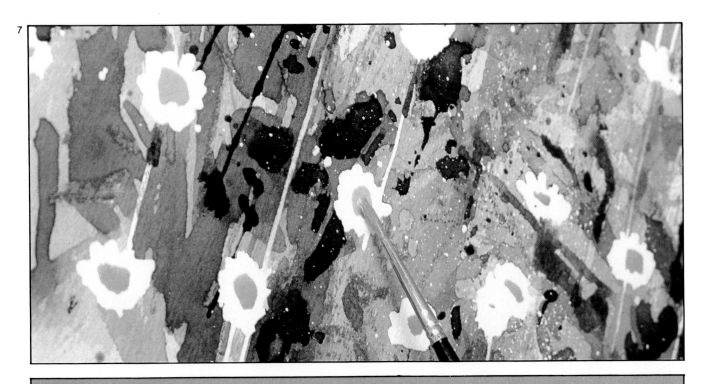

Field of Daisies

CHAPTER EIGHT

PORTRAIT AND FIGURE

*John Frederick Lewis' paintings were often of Middle-Eastern
subjects. Like many 19th-century painters he travelled
widely in search of inspiration. He was attracted by the rich
colours and textures of the East and in* The Harem *he
rendered their bright, jewel-like quality in a painstaking
technique typical of the watercolours of the period.*

ABOVE *This portrait,* Blowing Bubbles, *by Elaine Mills, was done from a photograph. The artist wished to capture the child in movement, not in a stiff, artificial looking pose. A scaled-up drawing made from the photograph was transferred to the painting surface by means of iron-oxide paper. The painting itself was built up in a series of thin washes, the colours kept light and clean throughout. The details of the face were done last, with the point of a No. 2 sable brush.*

A S MORE AND MORE ARTISTS SUCCUMB to the charms of watercolour, it is becoming an accepted medium for portraits and figure paintings, hitherto regarded as the province of oils. Its softness and translucence make it ideal for capturing the living qualities of skin and hair, but it needs particularly careful handling in this branch of painting if the surface is not to become muddy and dull. Accurate drawing is also vital, especially for portrait work. Try to draw from life wherever possible and avoid the temptation to put the paint on before the drawing is right.

♦ PAST AND PRESENT ♦ APPROACHES

Although artists have always used watercolour or pen-and-wash to make quick studies of faces and figures, there is really no tradition of portraiture in watercolour, and until this century paintings of the figure have also usually been in oil. The reasons for this have nothing to do with any inherent unsuitability of the medium itself. In the past

RIGHT *Edward Burra worked in watercolour because his severe arthritis made it difficult for him to handle oils. His use of the medium was truly amazing: he achieved a depth and richness of colour seldom seen in watercolour, and each detail was minutely described without ever appearing over-worked. In paintings such as* Harlem *(1934) Burra's concern was with the general atmosphere and lifestyle of the people he encountered, and his juxtaposition of dark and light colours and harsh and soft textures is highly descriptive.*

4. When the pencil drawing was complete the artist began to draw with the brush, painting in the shadow below the top eyelid. The eyes are the focal point of most portraits and need very careful treatment.

5. The next step was to get rid of some of the white paper by applying a pale wash to the background. A No. 2 sable brush was used to work on separate areas right across the painting.

7. Here the artist paints the darkest part of the hair, using a No. 2 sable brush and a mixture of violet, Payne's grey and Indian red. The hair had hitherto been mainly yellow ochre with touches of Indian red.

6. The stripes of the blanket were intensified before any further work was done on the face, as this was a very important part of the painting and acted as a key for the colours and tones of the face and hair.

8. By this stage the paper had been entirely covered, but the painting was somewhat weak and insubstantial, the flesh tones too pale and cool. The artist therefore intensified all the tones, adding warmth to the flesh and giving a more solid feel to the face. The final touches were to paint in the pattern of the blanket and add definition to the hair, so that it formed a pleasing pattern without being fussy.

MATERIALS USED

- ♦ SUPPORT: pre-stretched Bockingford paper, measuring 18 × 16 in/45 × 40 cm.
- ♦ COLOURS: Indian red, yellow ochre, violet, Payne's grey, cobalt blue, ultramarine, alizarin crimson, cadmium red and sap green.
- ♦ BRUSHES AND OTHER EQUIPMENT: Nos. 6 and 2 sable brushes, a mechanical lead-holder and a putty rubber.

Against a Striped Blanket

◆ PORTRAIT OF PAUL ◆

This sensitive study is much more graphic in approach than the previous portrait. The artist is more interested in line than in colour, and has used a technique which is a combination of drawing and painting, enabling her to express the character of the sitter in a way she found suited his thin, somewhat aquiline, features.

She used a quill pen made from a goose feather, a drawing tool much favoured by such artists as Rembrandt, but the medium was dilute watercolour instead of the more traditional ink. A quill pen produces a less mechanical line than a metal nib, because strokes of different thicknesses can be made by turning the quill. By this means, and by varying the strength and colours of the paint itself, the artist has produced a series of contrasting lines — some thick and soft, some short and stabbing, and some fine and taut. She used a Chinese brush in combination with the quill, both to lay washes across the whole image and to soften the line in places by dipping it in a little clean water. Using watercolour gives an artist more freedom to modify or alter lines.

1. A simple pose, seen directly from the front, was chosen for the painting, because it gave the artist the opportunity to explore fully the lines and contours of the features. No preliminary pencil drawing was made, since the painting was in itself a drawing, which could be corrected as the work progressed.

2. This photograph shows how the artist varied the strength of the watercolour when drawing with the quill. She used three different mixtures: raw sienna and cobalt blue; Prussian blue and cadmium red; and yellow ochre and cadmium yellow.

3. Here the artist has found that she is not satisfied with the line of the cheekbone; so she lightens it with a brush dipped in water before re-drawing it.

4. A Chinese brush was used to apply small areas of colour all over the image. No attempt was made to render the colours precisely; they were applied in a spontaneous manner to create an overall effect.

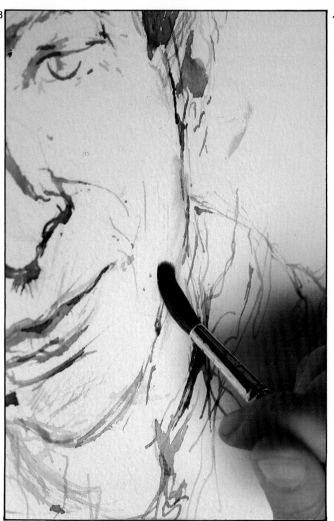

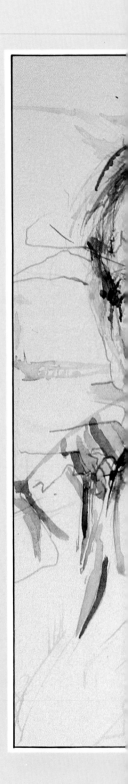

5. The artist has made little use of the traditional watercolour technique of flat washes. Instead, she has allowed the brushmarks to become part of the painting. The background was applied with two different brushes, a No. 9 sable round and a Chinese brush.

6. Once the lines had been firmly established and the artist was satisfied with the drawing, she laid a loose wash over the face and neck to build up the form and add warmth to the flesh.

Portrait of Paul

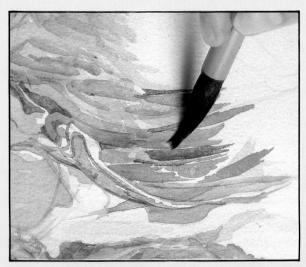

Although colour is not the most important aspect of the painting, it has been used boldly and sensitively. Here the artist is using a Chinese brush to apply small patches of bright colour to the clothing and darker tones to the hair.

MATERIALS USED

♦ SUPPORT: Langton watercolour paper with a Not surface, measuring 12 × 10 in/ 30 × 25 cm.
♦ COLOURS: raw sienna, cobalt blue, Prussian blue, cadmium red, cadmium yellow and yellow ochre.
♦ BRUSHES AND OTHER EQUIPMENT: A No. 9 sable round, a Chinese brush and a goose-feather quill pen.

CHAPTER NINE

STILL-LIFE

*Pierre Joseph Redouté was primarily a flower painter, official
artist to Marie Antoinette and later to the Empress Josephine.
His detailed flower studies are well known to us through
prints; his watercolours and drawings of other subjects are
much rarer, though equally fine. This still life, done in 1834,
towards the end of his life, shows a wonderfully fresh and
skilful handling of watercolour.*

STILL-LIFE as its name implies, simply means a composition of objects which are not moving and which are incapable of doing so, usually arranged on a table; the French rather depressingly call it 'dead life' (*nature morte*).

The subjects can be whatever you like, but traditionally the objects in a still-life group are in some way associated with each other — a vase of flowers with fruit, a selection of vegetables with cooking vessels or implements, and sometimes dead fish, game or fowl with a goblet of wine, perhaps, or a bunch of parsley. (Culinary still-lifes are less popular nowadays, possibly because they run the risk of looking like the cover of a cookery book.) Good paintings can be made from quite homely subjects. Vincent Van Gogh (1853-90) made a wonderful and moving still-life from nothing but a pile of books on a table.

Most artists have painted still-lifes at one time or another, and several, notably Jan Vermeer (1632-75), included them in their figure paintings. In the 17th century a group of Dutch artists became obsessed with still-life to the exclusion of all other subjects, and vied with one another to produce ever more lavish portrayals of table-tops gleaming with edible produce, rare porcelain and golden goblets. In many of these, tiny insects are visible among the foliage, blood drips from the mouths of freshly killed hares or rabbits, and bunches of grapes shine with tiny droplets of moisture, every object painted with breathtaking skill.

Because the subject of a still-life painting can be entirely controlled by the artist, as can its arrangement and lighting, still-lifes present an unusual opportunity for exploring ideas and experimenting with colour and composition. The greatest master of the still-life, Paul Cézanne (1839-1906), found that the form allowed him to concentrate on such fundamental problems as form and space and the paradox of transferring the three-dimensional world to a two-dimensional surface.

The ability to control the subject of a still-life means that you can take as much time as you like to work out the composition and complete the preliminary drawing, and you can practise painting techniques at leisure, trying out new ones as you feel inspired. Oddly, watercolour was seldom used in the past for still-lifes other than flower paintings, but it is now becoming extremely popular.

♦ SETTING UP A STILL LIFE ♦

There are no specific problems in painting a still-life or flower piece once it has been set up. The real challenge is arranging it, and this may take some time — plonking an assortment of objects down on a table will not give you a good painting. The wisest rule to follow at first is to keep the composition simple. The more objects you have the more difficult it is to arrange them in a harmonious way. It is also best to have a theme of some kind: if the various objects are too different in kind they will look uneasy together.

Start with something you like, a bowl of fruit on a patterned tablecloth, perhaps, or a pot plant, and keep arranging and re-arranging until you are satisfied that you have achieved a good balance of shapes and colours. Drapery is often used to balance and complement the main subject, and it is useful to have a selection of fabrics or tablecloths on hand for this purpose. Many artists make small sketches or diagrams to work out whether a vertical line is needed in the background, or a table-top shown as a diagonal in the foreground. Finally, when you are fairly sure that the arrangement will do, look at it through a viewing frame to assess how well it will fill the space

LEFT Cezanne used still-life to explore the relationships of forms and their interaction on various spatial planes. He usually worked in oils, but Still Life with Chair, Bottles and Apple, *shows his understanding of watercolour.*
ABOVE William Henry Hunt produced charming portraits as well as genre

subjects, using his paint rather dry to depict colours and textures with great accuracy. Plums *is an unusual approach to still life, as it has an outdoor setting but it was almost certainly done in the studio from preliminary sketches.*

allotted to it. Move the frame around so that you can assess several possibilities. Often you may find that allowing one of the objects to run out of the picture actually helps the composition.

Lighting is also very important. It defines the forms, heightens the colours and casts shadows which can become a vital component in the composition. If you are working by natural light other than a north light, it will, of course, change as the day wears on. This may not matter very much so long as you decide where the shadows are to be at the outset and do not keep trying to change them; but often it is more satisfactory to use artificial light. This solution sometimes brings its own problem, however, since if you are painting flowers or fruit they will wilt more quickly. You may simply have to decide which is the lesser evil.

♦ CYCLAMEN ♦

Flower arrangements are among the most popular of all still-life subjects. Indeed, they are often regarded as a separate branch of painting. In purely practical terms, however, they are a type of still-life, posing the same problems as well as sharing the major advantage of being a captive subject.

With any group of objects set up as a painting subject the main problem is arrangement, and hence the composition of the painting itself. Flowers in a vase, for example, do not always make a shape that fills a rectangle very well; so it is sometimes necessary to add other elements, such as

a plate, some fruit or background drapery. Here the composition is simple but very effective: the table-top, with its checked cloth, provides foreground interest to balance the pattern formed by the flowers themselves against the plain background. It also adds to the impression of solidity and its intersecting diagonal lines provide a pleasing contrast with the curved shapes. Interestingly, the tablecloth was added as an afterthought, when the artist had already painted the flower and pot; without it the character of the painting would have been quite different. When arranging a still-life or flower piece it is helpful to make a few advance sketches, as alterations cannot always be made as easily as they were here.

1. A careful outline drawing was made of the flowers and pot, and then the flowers were painted in with a mixture of cadmium red and purple lake. Particular attention was paid to the arrangement of the spaces created by the flowers against the background.

2. The mid-to-light tones of the leaves in the centre were laid on quite freely, sharper definition being reserved for those at the sides, to form a clear, sharp outline. The colours — emerald green, sap green, Payne's grey and a touch of raw sienna — were put on wet and allowed to mix on the paper.

3. The leaves and flowers were darkened in places and a first wash was then laid on the pot. Here, too, the colours were applied wet and moved around on the paper until the artist was satisfied with the way they had blended together.

4. A very pale wash was put on the underside of the dish, leaving the rim white to stand out against the checks. The blue used was chosen to echo the blue on the pot, and the shadow was added later.

FREEDOM AND LIGHT

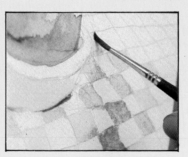

5. Here the artist is using the tip of a sable brush to paint the blue checks. Although they were painted carefully, and varied in size and colour to suggest recession, the artist has not attempted to produce perfectly straight or regular lines, which would have looked mechanical and monotonous.

6. The wet-into-wet technique was used for painting the pot, giving it a lively appearance suggestive of light and texture. Widely varying colours were applied with plenty of water and blended into one another. If the paint is too wet, or blends in the wrong way, it can be dabbed off with a sponge or tissue.

MATERIALS USED

♦ SUPPORT: pre-stretched watercolour paper with a Not surface, measuring 12 × 16 in/30 × 40 cm.
♦ COLOURS: cadmium red, alizarin crimson, raw sienna, purple lake, emerald green, sap green, lemon yellow, ultramarine, cobalt blue and Payne's grey.
♦ BRUSHES: Nos. 7 and 3 sable.

Cyclamen

◆ STILL LIFE WITH FRUIT ◆

The artist has used a number of different techniques to give a lively look to this bright fruit and vegetable group. His approach was unusual too, since he began by painting in the basic colours of the fruit, leaving the background and the table unpainted until a relatively late stage. This artist frequently paints piece by piece in this way, instead of adopting the more usual method of working all over the painting at the same time. It can be very successful, as it is here, but it does rely on the ability to judge tones and colours very accurately and upon having a clear idea of how the painting is to look finally.

A watercolour containing small, intricate shapes like these requires some planning, as too much overpainting and overlapping of colours can result in a muddy, tired-looking painting in which the brilliance of the colours is lost or diminished. In this case, the artist has solved the problem by using the watercolour mixed with white gouache, which gives it extra covering power without dulling the colours.

Once the colours of the fruit had been established, the warm ochre of the table top was laid on. The paint was applied around the shapes of the fruit, but quite boldly and loosely without too much concern about occasional overlapping. Texture was given to the wood by spattering opaque paint from a stiff brush and then by dragging the same brush, used rather dry, along the surface to suggest wood grain. The fruit was worked up and given more colour and form, and then the near-black background was painted in, giving an even richer glow to the fruit and providing a diagonal which balances the composition and brings all the elements in the painting together.

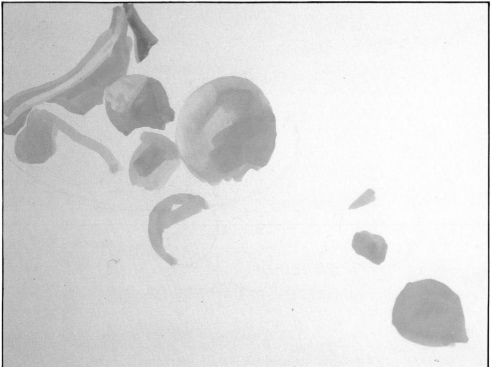

1. The artist begins by painting the lemons, using watercolour mixes with just a little white gouache.

2. By painting all the yellow areas first the artist has to a large extent established the composition. The pattern formed by the yellow shapes, interspersed with darker or more vivid forms and colours, is an important element in the painting.

3. Here the artist is working wet into wet to build up the forms and colours. Because he is using semi-opaque paint, he is able to lay a lighter yellow on top of the deep orange.

4. Now all the colours of the fruit have been laid on, although not in their final form. This enables the artist to gauge the colour and tone he needs for the table top.

ADDING TEXTURE

5. Having laid on the basic colour for the table top, taking it around the edges of the fruit, the artist now uses the spatter method to give a slight textural interest.

6. The grain of the wood is suggested by dragging a stiff, broad brush over the surface, using a darker colour in a slightly dry mixture.

7. This detail shows how well the solidity of the fruit has been depicted, being built up with quite broad and bold areas of colour. The dark shadows beneath them anchor them to the horizontal plane of the table.

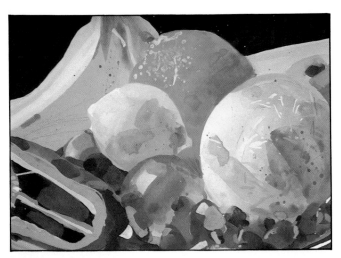

8. The addition of the black background gives a further sparkle to the clear, bright colours of the fruit. The textured highlights on the top of the orange were made by dribbling wet, opaque white paint from the brush on top of the darker colour.

9. The finished painting shows how important the greatly angled diagonal formed by the back edge of the table is to the composition. It balances the opposing diagonal formed by the group of fruit itself, a triangle with the bowl as the apex.

MATERIALS USED

♦ SUPPORT: plain white mounting board
♦ BRUSHES: Nos. 2, 7 and 9 sables and a 1-in/2.5 cm bristle brush
♦ COLOURS: lemon yellow, cadmium yellow, cadmium red, alizarin crimson, sap green, cobalt blue, raw umber and ivory black.

Still Life with Fruit

GLOSSARY

ALLA PRIMA A direct method of painting in which an image is developed in wet pigment without reliance on preliminary drawing or underpainting.

AQUEOUS A term which refers to a pigment or medium soluble, or capable of being suspended, in water.

BINDER A medium which can be mixed with powder pigment to maintain the colour in a form suitable for painting or drawing. For example, gum is the binder used for making both watercolour paint and pastel sticks. Oil binders produce materials with different properties.

BLOCKING IN The technique of roughly laying out the forms and overall composition of a painting or drawing in terms of mass and tone or colour.

BODY COLOUR Paint, such as gouache, which has opacity and therefore covering power. In watercolour this can be achieved by adding white to eliminate transparency. Body colour may be used to add highlights or colour.

BROKEN COLOUR This is an effect achieved by using colours in a pure state, without blending or mixing them, and dragging paint of a stiff quality across the support so that previous layers can be seen through the new application.

CALLIGRAPHIC A term referring to a linear style of painting or drawing characterized by flowing, rhythmic marks.

CHARCOAL A drawing material made by reducing wood, through burning, to charred, black sticks. All charcoal tends to powder but sticks are available in different thicknesses so the qualities in a charcoal drawing can be varied.

CHIAROSCURO This term literally means 'light-dark' and originally was used in reference to oil paintings with dramatic tonal contrasts. It is now more generally applied to work in which there is a skilfully managed interplay of highlight and shadow.

COMPLEMENTARY COLOURS There are three basic pairs of complementary colours, each consisting of one primary and one secondary colour. These are opposite colours in that the primary is not used in mixing the secondary, thus blue and orange (red mixed with yellow) are complementary colours. On an extended colour wheel, a warm red-orange is opposite green-blue.

COMPOSITION The arrangements of various elements in painting or drawing, for example, mass, colour, tone, contour etc.

CROSS HATCHING A technique of laying an area of tone by building up a mass of criss-cross strokes rather than with a method of solid shading.

DRY-BRUSH A means of applying watercolour with a soft, feathery effect by working lightly over the surface with a brush merely dampened with colour. The hairs may be spread between finger and thumb.

EARTH COLOURS A range of pigments derived from inert metal oxides, for example, ochres, siennas and umbers.

FERRULE The metal section of a paintbrush which holds the hairs.

FIGURATIVE This term is used in referring to paintings and drawings in which there is a representational approach to a particular subject; as distinct from abstract art.

FORESHORTENING The effect of perspective in a single object or figure, in which a form appears considerably altered from its normal proportions as it recedes from the artist's viewpoint.

FUGITIVE COLOUR Certain pigments are inherently impermanent or the colour may fade due to the action of natural elements, especially sunlight. A paint or dye which is short-lived in its original intensity is known as fugitive.

GOUACHE A water-based paint made opaque by mixing white with the pigments. Gouache can be used, like watercolour, to lay thin washes of paint, but because of its opacity it is possible to work light colours over dark and apply the paint thickly.

GRAIN The texture of a support for painting or drawing. Paper may have a fine or coarse grain depending upon the methods used in its manufacture. Some heavy watercolour papers have a pronounced grain which can be exploited to acheive effects of highlights and broken colour in painting.

GRAPHITE A form of carbon which is compressed with fine clay to form the substance commonly known as 'lead' in pencils. The proportions of clay and graphite in the mixture determine the quality of the pencil, whether it is hard or soft and the density of line produced. Thick sticks of graphite are available without a wooden pencil casing.

GROUND The surface preparation of a support on which a painting or drawing is executed. A tinted ground may be laid on white paper to tone down its brilliance.

GUM ARABIC A water soluble gum made from the sap of acacia trees. It is used as the binder for watercolour, gouache and soft pastels.

HALF TONES A range of tones or colours which an artist can identify between extremes of light and dark.

HATCHING A technique of creating areas of tone with fine, parallel strokes following one direction.

HUE This term is used for a pure colour found on a scale ranging through the spectrum; that is red, orange, yellow, green, blue, indigo and violet.

IMPASTO A technique of applying paint thickly so that a heavy texture is discernible, created by brush or knife marks. Gouache, having more body than watercolour, is suitable for this technique and impasto is commonly used in oil painting.

LOCAL COLOUR The inherent colour of an object or surface, that is its instrinsic hue unmodified by light, atmospheric conditions or colours surrounding it. For example, a red dress, a grey wall.

MASKING A technique of retaining the colour of the ground in parts of a painting by protecting it with tape or masking fluid while colours are applied over and around the masked areas. The mask is peeled or rubbed away when the painting is dry. This practice gives the artist freedom to work over the whole surface without losing shapes or areas of highlight.

MEDIUM This term is used in two distinct contexts in art. It may refer to the actual material with which a painting or drawing is executed, for example, gouache, watercolour or pencil. It also refers to liquids used to extend or alter the viscosity of paint, such as gum or oil.

MODELLING In painting and drawing modelling is the employment of tone or colour to achieve an impression of three-dimensional form, by depicting areas of light and shade on an object or figure.

MONOCHROME A term describing a painting or drawing executed in black, white and grey only, or with one colour mixed with white and black.

NOT A finish in high quality watercolour papers which falls between the smooth surface of hot-pressed, and the heavy texture of rough paper.

OCHRES Earth colours derived from oxide of iron in a range from yellow to orange-red.

OPACITY The quality of paint which covers or obscures a support or previous layers of applied colour.

PALETTE The tray or dish on which an artist lays out paint for thinning and mixing. This may be of wood, metal, china, plastic or paper. By extension the term also refers to the range of colours used in making a particular image or a colour scheme characteristic of work by one artist.

PASTEL A drawing medium made by binding powder pigment with a little gum and rolling the mixture into stick form. Pastels make marks of powdery, opaque colour. Colour mixtures are achieved by overlaying layers of pastel strokes or by gently blending colours with a brush or the fingers. Oil pastels have a waxy quality and less tendency to crumble, but the effects are not so subtle.

PERSPECTIVE Systems of representation in drawing and painting which create an impression of depth, solidity and spatial recession on a flat surface. Linear perspective is based on a principle that receding parallel lines appear to converge at a point on the horizon line. Aerial perspective represents the grading of tones and colours to suggest distance which may be observed as natural modifications caused by atmospheric effects.

PICTURE PLANE The vertical surface area of a painting or drawing on which the artist plots the composition and arranges pictorial elements which may suggest an illusion of three-dimensional reality and a recession in space.

PIGMENT A substance which provides colour and may be mixed with a binder to produce paint or a drawing material. Pigments are generally described as organic (earth colours) or inorganic (mineral and chemical pigments).

PRIMARY COLOURS In painting the primary colours are red, blue and yellow. They cannot be formed by mixtures of any other colours, but in theory can be used in varying proportions to create all other hues. This is not necessarily true in practice, as paint pigments used commercially are unlikely to be sufficiently pure.

RESIST This is a method of combining drawing and watercolour painting. A wash of water-based paint laid over marks drawn with wax crayon or oil pastel cannot settle in the drawing and the marks remain visible in their original colour, while areas of bare paper accept the wash.

SABLE The hair of this small, weasel-like animal is used in making soft brushes of fine quality which are usually favoured by watercolour artists.

SCUMBLING A painting technique in which opaque paint is dragged or lightly scrubbed across a surface to form an area of broken colour which modifies the tones underneath.

SECONDARY COLOURS These are the three colours formed by mixing pairs of primary colours; orange (red and yellow), green (yellow and blue) and purple (red and blue).

SPATTERING A method of spreading paint with a loose, mottled texture by drawing the thumb across the bristles of a stiff brush loaded with wet paint so the colour is flicked onto the surface of the painting.

STIPPLING The technique of applying colour or tone as a mass of small dots, made with the point of a drawing instrument or fine brush.

STUDY A drawing or painting, often made as preparation for a larger work, which is intended to record particular aspects of a subject.

SUPPORT The term applied to the material which provides the surface on which a painting or drawing is executed, for example, canvas, board or paper.

TONE In painting and drawing, tone is the measure of light and dark as on a scale of gradations between black and white. Every colour has an inherent tone; for example, yellow is light while Prussian blue is dark, but a coloured object or surface is also modified by the light falling upon it and an assessment of the variation in tonal values may be crucial to the artist's ability to indicate the three-dimensional form of an object.

TOOTH A degree of texture or coarseness in a surface which allows a painting or drawing material to adhere to the support.

TRANSPARENCY A quality of paint which means that it stains or modifies the colour of the surface on which it is laid, rather than obliterating it. Watercolour is a transparent medium and colour mixtures gain intensity through successive layers of thinly washed paint. When an opaque paint like gouache is laid in this way the colours tend to be devalued or hidden.

UNDERPAINTING A technique of painting in which the basic forms and tonal values of the composition are laid in roughly, before details and local colour are elaborated. This was originally an oil painting technique where an image executed in monochrome was coloured with thin glazes, but the term has come to have a more general application.

VALUE The character of a colour as assessed on a tonal scale from dark to light.

WASH An application of paint or ink considerably diluted with water to make the colour spread quickly and thinly. Transparency is the vital quality of watercolour and ink washes, whereas gouache washes are semi-transparent.

WATERCOLOUR Paint consisting of pigment bound in gum arabic, requiring only water as a medium. Transparency is the characteristic of watercolour as compared with other types of paint and the traditional technique is to lay in light tones first and build gradually to dark areas.

WATERMARK The symbol or name of the manufacturer incorporated in sheets of high quality watercolour paper. The watermark is visible when the paper is held up to the light.

WET INTO WET The application of fresh paint to a surface which is still wet, which allows a subtle blending and fusion of colours. Watercolour artists often prefer to lay washes wet over dry so that a series of overlapping shapes creates the impression of a structured form.

INDEX

Page numbers in italic refer to captions.

A

aerial perspective, 43, 45, 58, *58–61*
Against a Striped Blanket, 105–6, *105–7*
Audubon, John James, 82

B

backgrounds, 39, 90, *90–3*
Blake, William, 10, 104
Bonington, Richard Parkes, 10 69
    Castelbarco Tomb, 69, *69, 70*
brights, *19*
brush work, *7, 8*, 30, *30*
brushes, 18–19, *18, 19*
    brights, *19*
    Chinese, 108, 109, 111, *111*
    fans, 18, *19*
    flats, 18
    rounds, 18, *19*
    sable, 18, *18*
Burne-Jones, Edward, 104
Burra, Edward, 103
    Harlem, 105, *105*

C

Cézanne, Paul, 116
    Still Life with Chair, Bottles and Apple, 116, *116*
Chinese brushes, 108, 109, 111, *111*
Church in France, 76–9, *76–9*
Clinch, Moira, 71
    Summer Pavilion, 71
Clouds, 66–7, *66–7*
cold–pressed papers, 16–17
colours, 14–15, *14*, 16, 43–7, *45*, 55, *55–7*, 120, *120–1*
    complementary, 45–6
    cool, *44, 45, 46*
    fugitive, 16
    the palette, 16, *22*
    pencils, 34
    warm, *44, 45, 46*
Complementary colours, 45–6
composition, 38–41, *38–40*, 72, *72–5*, 90,

90, 94, *94–5*, 118
Constable, John, 10, 50, 52
cool colours, *44, 45, 46*
Cotman, John Sell, 10, 52
    The Dismasted Brig, 10
    St. Benet's Abbey, 8
Cozens, John, 10
Crome, John, 52
Cyclamen, 118–19, *118–19*

D

Delacroix, Eugène, 10
Distant Hills, 58–61, *59–61*
'dragged' wash, 10
drawing, *40*, 41–2, *41–2*, 53, 104, 105, *105–7*, 108, *108–11*
drawing boards, 20, *21*, 22–3
dry-brush work, 30, *30*
Dürer, Albrecht, 10, 81, 82
    The Great Piece of Turf, 10, 82
    Young Hare, 81, *81*, 82

E

easels, 20–1, *20–1*
edges
    washing into, 28, *73*
equipment, 18–23
    accessories, 23, *23*
    brushes, 18–19, *18, 19*
    Chinese brushes, 108, 109, 111, *111*
    drawing boards, 20, *21*
    easels, 20–1, *20–1*
    palettes, 22–3, *22*
    pencils, 41–2, 90
    quill pens, 108, *108–11*
    satchels, *20*
    viewing frames, *39–40*

F

fans, 18, *19*
Field of Daisies, 96–9, *96–9*
figure painting, *38, 39*, 102–13, *103–13*
flat washes, 26–7, *26*
flats, 18
della Francesca, Piero, *38*
fugitive colours, 16

G

Gainsborough, Thomas, 50
Geranium, 94–5, *94–5*
Girl by a Window With a Blind, 112–13, *112–13*
    Girl in Armchair, 104
Girtin, Thomas, 10, 51
    The White House, Chelsea, *50*, 51
Golden Section, 38
gouache, 7, 9, 14, *15*, 34, 120, *120–3*
gradated washes, 28, *29*
gum water, 35

H

hand-made paper, 17
'high-key', 105, *105–7*
highlighting, 32, *33*, 35
history of watercolours, 9–10, 50, 52, 102, 103
hot-pressed paper, 16–17
Hunt, William Henry, 117
    Plums, 117, *117*
Hunt, William Holman, 30

L

landscapes, 50, *50–1*, 52–67, *52–4, 56–67*
Lewis, John Frederick, 101
    The Harem, 101, *101*, 104
light, 47, *112*, 113, *113, 118*
lighting, 22, 117
Lorraine, Claude, 50

M

masking, 30, 31, 32, 62, *63–4*, 96, *96*, 98, *98*
materials, 8–9, 32–4, *32*
    gum water, 35
    masking materials, 30, 31, 32
    paints, 7, 8–9, *13*, 14–16, *14–15*, 34, 89, *89*
    paper, 16–17, *16–17*
Michel, Sally, 82
    Ring-tailed Lemur, 82, *82–3*

Mills, Elaine
  Blowing Bubbles, 102, *102,* 104

N

Nash, John, 10
Nash, Paul, 10
natural history subjects, *81,* 82–99, *82–99*
negative space, 39

O

Old Harry and His Wife, 62–5, *62–5*
opaque paints, 89, *89*
outdoor work, 37, 38–9, 50, *50–1,* 52–67,
  52–4, 56–7, 69, 70–9, *71–9, 81,* 82–99,
  82–99

P

paints, 8–9, *13,* 14–16, *14–15*
  additives, 34
  colours, 14–15, *14,* 16, 43–7, *45,* 55,
    55–7, 120, *120–1*
  fugitive, 16
  gouache, *7, 9,* 14, *15,* 34
  opaque, 89, *89*
  packaging of, 14, *15*
  permanence of, 16
  poster colours, 14
  powder paints, 14
  semi-moist, 14, *15*
palettes, *22, 23*
Palmer, Samuel, 10
  The Magic Apple Tree, 7
paper, 16–17, *16*
  stretching, 17, *17*
pencils, 34, 41–2, 90
perspective, 42–3, *43,* 44, 45, 70–1, 76,
  76–9,
  aerial, 43, 45, 58, *58–61*
Pheasant, 90–3, *90–3*
photographs, 47, 52, 70, 104
Portrait of Paul, 108–11, *108–11*
portraits, 39, *41,* 102–3, *103–13*
poster colours, 14
Poussin, Nicolas, 50
powder paints, 14
problem-solving, *25,* 35

Q

quill pens, 108, *108–11*

R

Redouté, Pierre-Joseph, 82, 115, *115*
reference material, 47
  photographs, 47, 52, 70, 104
resist method, 32
rough paper, 17
rounds, 18, *19*
van Ruisdael, Jacob, 50

S

sable brushes, 18, *18*
Sandby, Paul, 10
satchels, *20*
seascapes, *49,* 50, 62, *62–5*
semi-moist paints, 14, *15*
Seurat, Georges, 31
spattering, 30, 31, *31*
sponge washes, 27, *27,* 67
still-life, 90–3, *90–3,* 115–23, *115–23*
Still Life With Fruit, 120–3, *120–3*
subjects
  arrangement of, 117, 118, *118–19*
  choice of, 53
Summer Painting, 55–7, *56–7*
Sutherland, Graham, 10

T

techniques, 8, 10, 25–47
  brush work, *7, 8,* 30, *30*
  composition, 38–41, *38–40,* 72, *72–5,*
    90, *90,* 94, *94–5,* 118
  highlighting, 32, *33,* 35
  masking, 30, 31, 32, 62, *63–4,* 96, *96,*
    98, *98*
  perspective, 42–3, *43,* 44, 45, 70–1,
    86, *76–9,*
  problem-solving, *25,* 35
  resist method, 32
  spattering, 30, 31, *31*

  textural, 30–31, *30–1,* 76, *76–9,* 97,
    97, 120–3, *120–3*
  tonal, 58–61, *58–61,* 105, *105–7*
  washes, 26–30, *28, 29, 34,* 55–67,
    56–7, 62–3, 66–7, 73–4, 76–7, 85–7,
    90–1, 95
  wet-into-dry, 85, *85–8*
  wet-into-wet, 85, *85–8,* 118, *118–19*
textural work, 30–31, *30–31,* 76, *76–9,*
  97, *97,* 120–3, *120–3*
tonal contrasts, 58–61, *58–61,* 105,
  105–7
tone, 43
topographical work, *69,* 70–9, *71–9*
Towne, Francis, 10, 53
  Grasmere by the Road, 52–3, 53
Tropical Fish, 85–9, *85–9*
Turner, Joseph Mallard William, 10, 50,
  52, 54,
  Study of Tintern Abbey, 70, *70*
  Venice from the Guidecca, 54, *54*

V

Van Gogh, Vincent, 116
variegated washes, *27,* 28, *29,* 30
Vermeer, Jan, 116
viewing frames, 39–40
Vineyard in Italy, 72–5, *72–5*

W

warm colours, *44, 45, 46*
washes, 26–30, *28,* 29, *34,* 55–66, *56–7,*
  62–3, 66–7, 73–4, 76–7, 85–7, 90–1,
  95
  'dragged', *10*
  edges of, 28, *73*
  flat, 26–7, *26*
  gradated, 28, *29*
  sponge, 27, *27,* 67
  variegated, 27, 28, *29,* 30
  wet-into-dry, 85, *85*
  wet-into-wet, 85, *85*
wax masking, 32
wet-into-dry technique, 85, *85–8*
wet-into-wet technique, 85, *85–8,* 118,
  118–19
Winer, Marc, *84*
de Wint, Peter, 10, 51
  Walton-on-Thames, 51

ARTISTS' CREDITS

Ian Sidaway pp 24, 30, 31, 32, 35, 38, 42 (left), 46 (top), 58–61, 62–65, 76–79, 90–99, 120–123; Elaine Mills pp 41, 102, 105–107; Stan Smith pp 40, 46 (bottom), 48, 72–75; Kate Gwynn p 53 (top right); Ann Verney pp 55–57; Mark Winer pp 66, 67, 84, 104, 118, 119; Sally Michel pp 83, 85–89; Jane Wisner pp 108–111; John Devane pp 112, 113.